TEENAGERS!

What every parent *has* to know

D0715270

TEENAGERS!

What every parent *has* to know

Rob Parsons

'In the battlefield that is the parenthood of teenagers, this book is not just
wonderfully enlightening, but strangely
comforting.'

Prima Magazine

HODDER

British Library Cataloguing in Publication Data
A record for this book is available from the British Library

ISBN 978 0 340 86276 6

Printed and bound in Great Britain by
Clays Ltd, St Ives plc

The paper and board used in this paperback are natural recyclable products
made from wood grown in sustainable forests. The manufacturing processes
conform to the environmental regulations of the country of origin.

Hodder & Stoughton
A Division of Hodder Headline Ltd
338 Euston Road
London NW1 3BH
www.madaboutbooks.com

To Katie for all the coffees, to Lloyd for
all the curries, and to Dianne for all the patience.
Thank you.

Contents

Acknowledgements

As ever, special thanks to Sheron Rice who has exhibited patience and commitment way beyond the call of duty. And to Jonathan Booth, Wendy Bray, Samantha Callan and Jonathan Mason. And then to everybody else who helped, including Michael Bates, Anne Carlos, Dave Carlos, Emma Coffey, Paul Francis, John Gallacher, Kate Hancock, Dave Lumsdon, Sarah Mason, David McKie, Pete Mortimer, Paula Pridham, Steve Williams, and all the team at Care for the Family.

And thank you to my editor Judith Longman and all the team at Hodder & Stoughton and to my agents Eddie Bell and Pat Lomax of the Bell Lomax Agency.

Before we start

Sarah remembers the conversation well: it was in the ante-natal class and the midwife asked the mums-to-be if they had any preferences with regard to pain relief. There were twelve in the class: nine first-time mums like Sarah herself, two with toddlers, and Hilary who was in her forties and for whom this pregnancy was something of a surprise – she already had two grown-up children. It was Hilary who spoke first: 'Yes, I do have a preference. I'd like the strongest painkillers you've got – and ideally something that doesn't wear off until the child hits twenty!' The midwife frowned and the others in the class just couldn't understand what the older woman meant. But Sarah never forgot the incident. In fact, fifteen years later in the middle of the tough times, it sustained her because she knew that she was not alone. Out there somewhere was a mother who had worn the 'I've got a teenager' tee-shirt and come out the other end still sane and even laughing at it all. Sarah had a soul-mate.

Over the past twenty years or so I have spoken to hundreds of thousands of parents in seminars. Sometimes at the end of those events people will come to the front of the auditorium to chat. We have conversations about many aspects of family life, but questions and comments about teenagers beat everything else by ten to one. As I talk with those parents, many seem to be going through the same emotion: fear.[1] And I sympathise.

There are at least three occasions when I have been scared out of my life. One occurred somewhere over the Atlantic Ocean at thirty-five thousand feet, involved a hundred-and-ninety-six-ton jumbo 747 and lasted for twenty seconds. The second happened in a Malaysian jungle, with some wild animals who it seemed had decided to eat me, and lasted for five minutes. And the third involved two teenage children and seemed to last for the best part of ten years. I guarantee that if you had been in seat number 35H on the Continental Airlines Flight to Denver, you too would have been scared. And I feel sure that as the animals advanced towards you on that hot summer's day you, like me, would have yelled for help. But if you have never had a teenager, you could never under-stand the sheer fear, bewilderment and mystery of feeling, 'Children I signed up for, but who are these?'

If fear is a common experience of many parents of teenagers, then it's also true that many also go through another emotion: anxiety. One mother put her experience of the teenage years like this:

> *I just didn't expect it. Until he was twelve, Tom used to cuddle up to me on the sofa as we watched television together. I even began to worry that he was a bit too clingy. I can tell you that 'clingy' is not a problem now. He can only just bring himself to talk to me – and then he looks as if he's just discovered me on the bottom of his shoe. And what really hurts is to see him come to life on the phone with his friends. And then there's the sheer worry. I worry all the time. And the level of worrying has rocketed. When he was small, I'd worry if he wasn't walking or talking fast enough, or whether his*

reading was up to scratch, but suddenly I'm worrying that he's going to do something that will ruin his whole life. I know he's trying to be independent and all this is a learning process, but I'm his mother . . . and I know it sounds pathetic, but I just can't help myself.

She's not alone. In his study of parenthood, historian Peter Stearns claims that the defining character of contemporary American parenthood is anxiety.[2] He also argues that today's parents are more worried about their own competence than parents in the past and says there has been a very real drop in parents' self-confidence.

At the heart of so much of this worry is a sense that now we can't protect them in the same way as when they were small. When they were six we could usually make them do what we felt was best – even if it involved a little bribery! But as the teenage years progress we realise we no longer have that kind of control – and, in our better moments, don't even want it (though that doesn't stop the experience being terrifying). And for many of us, all this is a bit of a surprise. After all, we've been pretty good parents and although we'd heard the stories of trauma in other families, we'd always thought that when it came to our turn, a slight tweaking of what had already worked with our pre-teens would do the trick. For many parents (not all by a long way!) the first ten or twelve years or so of their children's lives are reasonably calm, with occasional moments of turbulence. But for some families, things are about to get a lot more interesting. One father, looking back on the experience, put it like this:

> *It is as if the family is in a small boat, drifting down a quiet river. Some days there are storms and you need to batten down the hatches; there are occasional dangers, but generally the journey is smooth. And then one day it happens: the realisation dawns on you that one of the kids is not in the boat any more! In fact, he's somehow now got a boat of his own and is fifty metres downstream waving at you. You can't work out whether he's saying 'Help me!' or 'Goodbye'. And as if that wasn't bad enough, you have just passed a sign reading 'Dangerous rapids ahead!' Within moments both boats are rocking violently. Almost all your*

energies are taken up just trying to keep your own boat afloat and yelling warnings of impending rocks to your teenager.

Now it is true that for some families the rapids are both short and tame; their teenagers sail through without too much trouble. But for others the experience of the first twelve years is about to be reversed. The forecast is now for total turbulence with occasional moments of calm – during which you are so tired you probably miss them anyway.

But why are the rapids such a surprise? And is there any way to avoid them? I have been asked that question in different ways by parents all over the world who were really asking, 'Where did we go wrong?' or 'Having seen what's happened to our friends' kids, how can we do things differently?' The short answer is that with most teenagers there's not a lot you *can* do. So is all lost? Is the best plan to buy a thousand tins of beans, some bottled water and hunker down under the stairs until they come out the other end in their early twenties? At times, most of us have wished with all our hearts that we had taken that option, but we didn't – because it really isn't one: we are their parents. They may say they hate us, call us un-cool, and compare us unfavourably with the parents of their best friend, but on us lies the awesome responsibility of getting them through the teenage years. And that's where this book comes in. Its main aim is a straightforward one: to help 'get them through'.

But before we begin, a word of realism. I have worked for twenty years with a national charity in the area of family life and for thirty years with a community centre on a vast housing estate. Those experiences have done at least two things for me. First, they have stopped me taking myself too seriously as an author – the vast majority of parents in the world today have never seen a book on parenting, never mind read one, and they manage to get by just fine. Second, I know that some parents' experiences with their teenagers do not come within the scope of a book like this. Their children may be physically violent – sometimes to the parents themselves – verbally abusive, or addicted to illegal drugs, perhaps even stealing from those who love them to fund their habit. These parents live their daily lives in what at times feels like a war zone. They have lost count of the times they have attended school meetings with irate head teachers, been called to police stations, or sat in the casualty department of hospitals. If this is an experience you are going through, I don't want you for a minute to think that I believe a short book – or even a long one for that matter – can solve all your problems, but I hope that even in your situation you may find something here that helps.

Through my seminars and writing I have had the privilege of interacting with parents from Bournemouth to Beijing. Having had countless conversations with distraught mothers and at-the-end-of-their-tether fathers, and sometimes with their children, I have become convinced that the greatest need parents have today is not for answers. I say the *greatest* need because, without doubt, answers are important: we need to know how to best communicate with our teenagers, when and how to set boundaries, and how to help them get through the rapids without experiencing shipwreck on the way. But by far the deepest need is to know that whatever we are experiencing, we are not alone.

Let's start there.

1

You are not alone

One psychologist likened the teenage experience to the launch of a spacecraft. With twelve years or so of training behind him, a pubescent boy makes his way to the launch pad. He climbs aboard 'Adolescent One' as his mother and father bite their nails back at Mission Control. Suddenly the great engines roar into life and they watch as Darren makes his way into the stratosphere. And then the strangest thing happens: they lose all contact with the spaceship. His mother is beside herself. He had promised to ring when he got to the moon, and anyway has he forgotten he's got a dental appointment next Tuesday? But there is no communication: nothing. Well, not exactly nothing: the radio operator allows the parents to listen in and they just about pick up what sound like grunts – though nobody can decipher them. The years go by, until a whole decade has passed and then suddenly – signals from outer space! He's still alive! And even more remarkably, he has discovered the power of speech again – whole sentences are tumbling out. The parents rush back to Mission Control just in time to see his capsule burst into earth's atmosphere. All their fears are over: Darren is back!

But when did parenting become so traumatic? Typical comments I hear from parents of teenagers are: 'I'm a failure,' 'I don't know how to communicate with my teenager,' 'I'm overwhelmed with the responsibility of it all,' and, perhaps most commonly, 'I'm just so tired.' Did previous generations of parents worry as much? I doubt it. I had a good mother and father. They provided for me and my sisters; they tried to pass their values on to us; they loved us. They both died some years ago, but sometimes when I have been consumed with worry over my kids, I have imagined asking them a question: 'Did you worry about parenting us?' Of course, I can't guarantee what their reply would have been, but my guess is: 'To be honest, we rarely gave it a thought.'

Why is there such a difference in the perceptions

of parents just fifty years apart? The answer is that the world has changed. Grandparents sometimes say to me, 'Why do we make such a big deal about teenagers nowadays? People of my generation got through it without too much trouble.' OK, let's talk about 'people of my generation'. One psychologist, now in his sixties, put it like this:

When I was a teenager it was as if I was walking down a corridor with doors either side. The doors had labels: 'Alcohol', 'Gambling', 'Sex', 'Drugs'. But all the doors were locked. Occasionally I would hear of one of my friends who had gone through one of the doors into one of the rooms, but if that happened it was a big deal.

And then he went on to say this:

Today's teenager walks down that same corridor, but all the doors are open – and their friends are in the rooms shouting out, What are you doing out there? Come on in!

This is not just the ranting of some old timer longing for the golden years. Consider just one of those 'rooms'. Among children in England aged eleven to fifteen, alcohol consumption more than doubled during the 1990s[1] and research from the Royal Liverpool Children's Hospital shows a ten-fold increase between 1985 and 1996 in the number of children under fifteen admitted to hospital with acute alcohol poisoning.[2] Andrew McNeill of the Institute of Alcohol Studies calls the phenomenon, 'An epidemic of binge drinking'.[3]

These kinds of changes put enormous pressure on the parents of teenagers. But before we use all our emotion up on the difficulties of parenting, let's spare a thought for the teenagers themselves. One boy explained it like this: 'I hear older people say, "Youth is wasted on the young." Well, I want to tell you that it's not so great.'

I think he's right. Teenagers are at a stage where all the old certainties seem to be shaken. Various parts of their body, which hitherto have behaved reasonably well, now seem determined to do their own thing. It's unfortunate that at this time of life, when looking cool is paramount, their bodies seem determined to embarrass them by changing so fast. More than any-thing else, teenagers want to be accepted. They desperately want to look good. If they are girls, their role models tend to be slim and beautiful; if they are boys, their heroes are tall and muscular. The number one desire of teenage girls is to be thinner and for boys it is to be taller. At such a time the cruelty of peers can be devastating. They may be desperate for a boyfriend or girlfriend – and for many teenagers the trauma involved in this is almost unbearable.

And then there are the pressures of exams. I know that we've all had to go through this, but the modern education system is relentless in its continual testing and targets. Teenagers know they are in a competitive world and feel the pressure not to mess their lives up. How are you supposed to answer the question, 'What do you want to do when you grow up?' when you're not even sure whether you dare start shaving or not? (Perhaps they shouldn't be too worried: some of the most interesting adults I know of, at forty years plus, don't know what they want to do with their lives!)

Sixteen-year-old Gareth put it like this:

I'm battling to please my parents, my teachers and my friends and everything is so hypocritical. People say, 'Work hard, so you'll get a good job,' but loads of people I know with degrees are unable to really use them. Adults go on about under-age drinking, but we all know that alcopops are targeted at us. They say 'Plan for the future,' but if they go on blowing everybody up there's not going to be one.

Nicole, aged fifteen, said:

When I was little I only cried if I was hurt or I wanted something. I honestly feel like crying all the time now because of so many pressures.

We ought not to be too quick to dismiss all this as a lack of backbone in the young. The world they have to live in is a world we have created for them.[4] And many of them are finding it just too hard. In 1995 more teenagers and young adults died from suicide than from cancer, heart disease, AIDS, pneumonia, influenza, birth defects and strokes combined.[5]

In such a world what we most need as parents is to get alongside each other, to offer mutual support and help get each other through,[6] but many modern parents experience the opposite: isolation.[7]

The other day my wife, Dianne, and I went to an architectural reclamation depot – a scrap yard for old houses. It was a fascinating place with piles of stained glass windows, fabulous fireplaces, weird and wonderful chandeliers, and garden furniture from a bygone age. As we strolled around we came upon a huge shed full of old front doors. I gazed at them and found myself wondering what stories they could tell – what joys, triumphs and fears had been lived out behind those doors. Isolation is one of the great tragedies of modern life. With few people to share with openly, we come to believe that what our family is going through – especially with our children – is unique. We make our evaluation of our circumstances behind the closed doors of our own home. We marry, procreate and handle death in isolation. That is not to say we are not surrounded by others who are tying the knot, raising kids and dealing with bereavement. It's just that we tend not to talk about these things any more.

Several things have conspired to lead to this situation. First is the breakdown of the extended family. The idea that fifty or so years ago dozens of family members lived under one roof is a myth, but people did tend to lead their lives close to relatives[8] – often in the same street. And that meant that experiences and accrued wisdom could be shared.

The second ingredient that makes isolation more likely is the sheer busyness of modern life. We hardly have time to see our husband or wife,[9] let alone take time to chat in depth with friends. I once saw a brilliant cartoon on a greetings card. It was of a mum driving a people carrier with a dozen seats in it. She was obviously just at the end of some mammoth taxi job and had deposited her children at a multitude of different activities. She looked weary, hassled . . . and puzzled. She was speaking to a small boy who was sitting alone in the otherwise empty vehicle: 'If Peter's at Cubs and Susan's at piano, Simon's at karate and Lucy's at ballet – who the heck are you?' Demos says that 'Caught between longer hours of work and ever more demanding parenting standards, it is often relationships which become the casualties of the time squeeze.'[10]

Third, we live in a competitive society where we can easily feel the need to present a face that says, 'We've got it all together.' Increasingly we live our lives behind our own front doors and carefully edit what we choose to show others. That's why, when marriages fall apart, friends so often say, 'We had no idea.' And it's also why, when asked how their kids are doing, many parents say, 'Fine,' but actually, within the four walls of their own home, they are breaking their hearts because they think this is 'just us'. Nearly half of all calls to Parentline Plus, the advice line for parents, cite isolation and loneliness as key concerns.[11]

But, of course, pressure on the family does not just show itself in the concerns of parents about children. Many teenagers cite as their main worry in life the fear that their parents will break up. Penny Mansfield, who heads up One Plus One, an organisation that has conducted in-depth research on family life over many years, says that, 'There is now compelling evidence that how parents get on – or don't get on – has a profound influence on their children's lives.'[12] This can even be the case in the later teenage years. Laura Telfer, a Relate counsellor for eighteen years, agrees that splitting up when the children are older can seem like an attractive option:

> There is definitely a susceptible time when the children leave home when all possibilities seem open. But it does not make the unexpected desertion any easier. What can be an exciting

venture for one partner is invariably a painful grieving episode for other family members. Children watch appalled as their family, that secure and safe place that survived all their childhoods, is swiftly dismantled.[13]

Anthropologist Margaret Mead, who studied family life across countless cultures worldwide said, 'Nobody has ever before asked the nuclear family to live all by itself in a box the way we do. With no relatives, no support, we're put in an impossible situation.'[14]

But it's not just the nuclear family; there is an especially strong need for single parents to know they are not alone.[15] I often meet single parents who say to me, 'I'm going through such a difficult time with my teenager.' They then relate the issues that I hear time and time again – perhaps rudeness, coming in late at night, alcohol, smoking or lack of interest in school. And as we talk, it's clear to me that the question they are really asking is, 'Is all this because I'm a single parent or is this normal with teenagers?' He or she simply has nobody with whom to talk.

I well remember a young mother telling me her story. She had three children – a boy of five, a girl of six, and a girl of eight. She said, 'My youngest son and older daughter are a delight, but the middle one, Annie, is ruining our lives. She tests me in every way, every single day of her life.' And then she paused and said, 'I know this is a terrible thing for a mother to say, but sometimes I don't feel I love her.' She lowered her head and began to cry. It was apparent this mother loved her child so much she would give her life for her.

I said, 'I hear this story from so many parents.'

She lifted her head, 'You do?'

'Yes,' I said. 'And I have two pieces of news for you. Let me give you the bad news first. If you have more than one child, you will almost certainly have at least one that tests you to the limit: Annie is yours. People will tell you that she'll grow out of it, but she probably won't. She is going to go on testing you not only now, but right through her teenage years.'

She forced a smile and said, 'Tell me the good news – quick!'

'It's normal,' I said. 'And there are things you can do that will not only lessen the trauma, but make it possible that one day you will have a relationship with this child that now you can only dream of.'

We talked for a while and then she left. When she was a little way down the aisle she turned and called back, 'Thank you so much.' As I watched her make her way to the exit through a deserted auditorium, I thought, 'Thank you for what?' – after all, she still had no detailed strategy to solve her problem. But perhaps she was thanking me for two precious gifts: the assurance that she isn't alone in all of this – that thousands of parents are going through exactly the same experiences . . . and a little hope.

We've noticed a change in her just lately. It's not that she doesn't love us, just that, as far as she can see, she doesn't need us. It's as if we don't matter as much to her now. She literally turns her back and walks away – not unkindly, just resolutely.

We know she still cares about us, but it's as if she doesn't want us to care about her. Our views don't matter, increasingly we 'don't understand'. She tells us we can't tell her what to do any more. She says, 'I'm not a child' and then behaves exactly like one. There is still that raw vulnerability. We see it creeping around the edges of her life when she thinks we're not looking.

It's as if she is being guided by a new force, a new leader. As if she has joined an invisible sect, which dictates all she should do and we have no part in it. Everything she does she wants to do by herself. Every decision must be made independently. There is nothing we can add.

She's wading out from the sheltered beach of childhood into the depths that are the sea of independence. She'll be a long way off out there and we won't be able to see how much she is splashing about. We just have to trust her to swim towards that horizon.

I want to tell her that we will still hold the life belt on the shore – just in case.

2

What's going on in your teenager's head

In the homes of many teenagers a single question echoes from the lips of parents: 'Why does he/she do that?' 'That' could refer to all kinds of behaviour. It could be that they seem to develop almost caveman-like characteristics and hibernate in their rooms with their music and their moods. It could be that they scream at you, 'I hate you for ruining my life.' As you ponder those words you find it hard to work out when all this 'ruining' occurred. So far as you can remember, you've changed nappies, taught them to read, got them to and from school, taken them to numerous doctors and, if they were boys, more casualty units than you can remember. In fact, at times you feel like screaming back, 'And I hate you, too – for ruining my life with your moods, your rudeness and your complete withdrawal of any hint of affection. And, while we're at it – for leaving a perfectly good pile of washed and ironed clothes on the floor in your room for a week and then giving them back to me walked over, sat on and creased to high heaven to wash again.'

For many years that question, 'Why does he/she do that?' has been answered by scientists with one word: 'hormones'. The testosterone and oestrogen coursing through our children's bodies got the blame for it all. And it's not hard to see why. We could at least observe what the chemicals were doing to our dearest; it was obvious that they were becoming sexual beings. During this stage the genital organs of both boys and girls enlarge, pubic hair grows, breasts grow in girls, and boys may develop temporary swellings under the nipples as production of testosterone increases. In boys the scrotal sac hangs lower and eventually the penis will increase in size, and, in a brilliant design feature, one testicle may hang lower than the other – usually the left – so that they don't bang into each other when walking!

Such physical development is not without com-plications. Have you ever wondered why teenagers are so awkward? The problem is that in puberty different parts of the body grow at different rates: you'd be awkward too if your head, hands and feet grew faster than the rest of you. It's true that the arms and legs try to catch up, but this just succeeds in giving that gangly look. The heart doubles in size, growth spurts occur – usually later in boys but much faster – and body weight for both boys and girls can double between the ages of ten and eighteen. In boys the shoulders broaden and girls put on a little extra fat around the hips and elsewhere too – which is why hormones may be to blame for that question asked in a million clothes-shop changing rooms: 'Mum, does my bum look big in this?'

So there it is – all explained by hormones – or rather there it *was*, until recent research changed the scene. Very few teenage brains have been available for post-mortem study compared to those of small children or elderly adults but, with the emergence of Magnetic Resonance Imaging (MRI), neuroscientists have been able to track the development of the teenage brain. Suddenly the whole picture of human development has changed. Neuroscientists had always assumed that the brain was fully formed by late childhood, but now it has become evident that different parts of the brain mature at different rates. The early pattern of brain growth, a surge in brain mass around ages two to three years, was already well established. Equally well attested was a process called myelination up to around age eight, whereby certain critical connections between neurons in the brain gain a fatty coating, which speeds transmission of signals. What MRI revealed was that in the early teenage years the brain undergoes another, previously unrecognised, growth spurt *at least the equal of the early childhood one.*[1] This explains a lot: any parent who has experienced *déjà vu* when faced with teenage tantrums – 'You are behaving like a two-year-old!' – may not be on entirely the wrong track. The 'terrible twos' and the 'traumatic teens' seem to have a very similar neural underpinning.

The research also showed that whereas the first round of myelination during the toddler years seems to relate to the individual's wiring for balance and movement, the second round focuses on areas of the brain devoted to memory and emotional reactions. The reason that being around some teenagers is similar to sitting at the base of an emotional Mount Etna is that their brains have not yet developed the full ability to control their emotions. The fact is that sometimes they can't help it very much when they are at their most infuriating. They are a work in progress: neither the child they were, nor the adult they will become.[2]

The last part of the development in the brain that occurs around this time has to do with the frontal lobes – the pre-frontal cortex immediately behind the forehead. This part of the brain is often referred to as 'the brain's policeman' or 'moral compass' and work is still generally in progress beyond the age of twenty. This means that not only the ability to control emotions, but the ability to make sound judgements[3] – to take a longer view and to postpone immediate gratification for the sake of longer-term gains – is limited.[4] This is why teenagers simply can't understand the logic of not going out with their friends tonight, so as to be fresh for the exam tomorrow: 'Dad! Tomorrow is like light years away!'

Chuck Nelson is a neuroscientist who spends much of his life trying to understand the complex development of the human brain. He says:

A lot of teenagers just don't see the consequences of actions. They don't think ahead. They don't see

27

that getting good grades today, for instance, makes a big difference to the person they will be later on. When they get older, they start to get that. And I think it has to do with the development of the brain, particularly the pre-frontal cortex, the part that controls working memory, inhibition, impulse control.[5]

He goes on to talk about the fact that some teenagers seem more muddled than eight-year-olds. But why? Surely an eight-year-old's pre-frontal cortex is less developed. Nelson says, 'Teenagers need to be independent from their parents. They want to be adults and they are exposed to a semi-adult culture. But they don't have the pre-frontal cortex to regulate those adult behaviours; they drink and they drive without seatbelts, all of that.' Dr Jay Giedd, another neuroscientist, put it like this: 'Teenagers have the passion and the strength, but no brakes, and they may not get good brakes until they are twenty-five.'[6]

And yet in the midst of all this, teenagers are at a time of their life when in some ways they are at their most generous and understanding of others. Unfortunately 'others' doesn't usually include their mother and father! For this reason they will willingly go on protests against the evils of global warming while leaving every light in the house on when they go out to join the march.[7]

Psychologist Anna Freud put it like this: 'Adolescents are excessively egoistic, regarding themselves as the centre of the universe and the sole object of interest, and yet at no time in later life are they capable of so much self-sacrifice and devotion.'[8]

The best word to describe many teenagers at this time is 'tentative'. Although they may present as arrogant, cocky and self-assured, inwardly they are desperately trying to make sense of their journey into independence. That puts a great responsibility on the adults around them – parents, teachers and youth workers. There will be occasions when all we want to do is puncture their 'know-it-all' attitude with a bit of sarcasm, but sometimes we'll have to bite our tongue and instead find ways to point them in the right direction without wrecking their sense of worth.

Apart from the teenager himself, parents take the main brunt of the pain of this growth into independence because they have been the source of the control – and frankly because most teenagers know that if they can experiment with anybody (for this read 'get away with it') it's with their parents; after all, the teenagers are learning on the job as well. But it doesn't mean that their characters have changed forever. Which is why, at the moment of your deepest despair, when you believe your child could have written the manual on rudeness, you will meet another parent in the supermarket who will say, 'I wish my son was more like yours. He's so polite; when he comes to tea, he always offers to help with the dishes.'

I'm not saying that getting to grips with what is going on with our teenagers' hormones and brains makes the painful times go away, but I'm sure they are a lot easier to deal with if we believe that not only are they not *our* fault, but in some ways they are not *their* fault either.

A mother approached me at the end of one of my parenting seminars. She'd obviously been crying and even now was finding it hard to speak. 'It's my son,' she said, 'I think he hates me.'

'Why do you think that?'

'Because he told me he did – and anyway he acts as if he does. He won't talk to me. If I ask him how school went, he just says, "Fine." If I ask him if he wants something to eat, he says he's not hungry – and then ten minutes later I see him raiding the fridge. If he sees me when he's out with his friends he won't acknowledge me. And if I try to hug him he practically has a seizure. I think I disgust him.'

I asked, 'Has it always been like this between you?'

'No. And that's what makes it so hard. Over the past year or so he's changed. We used to be so close. I know it sounds a bit soppy but he'd often hug me, and after school he'd follow me around the house telling me everything. I feel in some ways as if I've actually lost him. I think I'm grieving.'

This mother is observing from *outside*, the changes that are occurring *inside* her teenager. Both his brain and his body are telling him it's time to grow up and leave the child behind. That childhood stage was defined by parental control and therefore one of the dilemmas for him is how to break free of it. It's right that he undertakes this process, but it is likely to be clumsy and hurtful.

The woman in front of me was crying again. I touched her arm and said, 'I hear this all the time.'

She looked up. 'Really?'

'Yes,' I said, 'and particularly from mothers about their sons. There may be many reasons behind it, but one is that your son has just discovered sex.'

She looked alarmed.

'I don't mean he's sleeping around. I mean that out of a clear blue sky he's realised that girls attract him. More terrifyingly, he's noticing that when that attraction occurs, his body seems to have a life of its own. He's found that reciting algebraic equations calms it down a little, but not much and not for long.'

The thought of Ryan having an erection in his Maths class looked as though it might precipitate another flood of tears. I hurried on: 'So women attract him. The only problem is that the only woman he's ever really loved, and actually still does love, is his mother. And at the moment he's finding Geography difficult enough without trying to work out how to handle those kinds of emotions, so he falls back on what we all do when we feel emotionally unsure.'

'He pretends to reject me,' she said.

'Yes, and "pretends" is not a bad way of putting it. The truth is he doesn't know what's going on either – just that it's easier to keep you at a distance.

Sometimes he feels he wouldn't mind snuggling up on the sofa next to you as he used to, but he knows those days are gone. And it's not just boys who find this battle between what's going on in their brains and bodies confusing. I remember one teenage girl saying, "I sometimes think my body is way ahead of my brain. I spend half my time dreaming about boys and the other half wishing I could be back in the playground with my friends playing our old silly games."'

The woman smiled, 'I remember those days myself,' she said. 'But why is Ryan so rude to me?'

'Look, I'm not saying you should allow him to be rude to you. But understanding two things may help: first, it's not personal, and second, it will pass. Give him time. Don't turn your hurt back on him or force him to respond to you. Be patient and the day will almost certainly come when he is comfortable enough to hug you again. But that could be ten years down the road when he is secure in his own relationships. Those mothers who have bitten their tongues when there was so much they wanted to say, and hung in there waiting for the ice to melt, tell me it's worth waiting for.'

She smiled and said, 'Thank you. I feel so relieved.

You have no idea what this means to me.' But I think I do. Another mother put it like this:

> If you have a teenager who is behaving badly it is easy to assume that you have bred someone who is a monster or that they hate you. But once you learn that much of their behaviour can be explained by something that is physical, temporary, inevitable and universal, it takes the pressure off. You lose some of the emotional grief that you feel when your teenager is giving you a hard time . . . because I know what's going on in her brain I just don't get so angry. It really does help.[9]

She's right; even a little understanding of hormones, brain cells, frontal lobe cortexes and left-hanging testicles can help you to realise that what your teenager is really saying is: 'Look, Mum, don't take all this personally – just help me get through.'

At first we found it hard to understand her total lack of perspective on anything that happens. Working for the GCSEs which will determine the rest of her life pales into insignificance against the preparation for Emily's party on Friday, or finding the perfect pair of earrings for Saturday night. She seems unable to think long term and lurches from one minor crisis – with friends, face or fad – to another. She always seems to be on the brink of the best. This party will do it, that night out clubbing, even that particular mascara. The next thing is always the best thing and the best thing is always going to happen tonight. Her life is about the short term; the long term can look after itself. It's now that matters most, tomorrow and next week only matter a bit more, and next year frankly seems an age away. Why worry about it?

But looking back we remembered being just the same. Living for the intensity of the moment. Smells and music 'take us back' and make us realise how emotionally charged those days were.

Life seemed more about who said what and what he or she might do than what we should be doing. The future, the serious stuff, did matter. It just didn't seem so urgent. We'd deal with it eventually. And she will too – deal with it eventually. There is nothing we can do to get her there faster. There's just too much happening, today.

The sad thing is, we tell ourselves that the best way to live is 'in the moment' and here we are trying to move her on to the next!

3

The testing teenager

Of all the great mysteries of life, surely one of the greatest must be that if you have at least two children you are going to get widely different personalities. This is a law of nature. It exists, I believe, to humble the parents of well-behaved, compliant children and stop them giving critical advice to every other mother or father in their road.

As with all laws of nature, there is an occasional aberration of this rule, and once in a while a parent is delivered two compliant children in succession. When this occurs it creates a parent so terrifying they should be banned from speaking to other adults at parent and toddler groups, school gates and Sports Days. These parents have children who seem truly perfect. When they are babies they not only sleep all night, but never defecate as soon as you change a nappy, preferring if possible to use the same one twice. In toddler-hood, whenever they feel queasy they always rush straight to the bathroom and wouldn't even think of throwing up down the back of the settee; they are a joy to take to the supermarket and squeeze your hand in appreciation of the trip as they pass other kids throwing tantrums in the aisles. But it's at school that these angels really come into their own. They use the cardboard from toilet rolls to make Blue Peter castles fit for royalty and write essays that have teachers rushing out to buy dictionaries. By the age of ten they have adopted several children from third-world countries to whom they regularly write letters and send a percentage of their pocket money – money that they earn by selling origami models made from the litter they collect on the way home from their trombone class.

Such children will later provide the literary fodder that will be used by their parents to depress their friends in Christmas family letters. In these, the progress of little George will be catalogued each year from 'Youngest toddler to walk in Epsom' through 'Most A-stars at GCSE for any child since the

Education Act of 1944' and culminating with the news that 'George at aged nineteen is consultant gynaecologist to the Queen.'

To the parents of these rare creatures I have only three pieces of advice. First, don't knock it – enjoy it! You are blessed. Second, keep quiet about your achievements. Don't assume it's because you're a great parent – you may have just got lucky. And third, don't even think of having another child.

But it's just possible that's not your situation right now. In fact, sometimes you catch yourself tearing out clumps of hair and screaming, 'Where did I go wrong?' It seems that your teenager has a life goal of testing his mother to distraction. If you have just one child, you may well think that all children are like this, but if your first child was compliant it is particularly hard. You were lured into the delusion that if you read all the stuff on parenting, bought the books, watched the programmes and simply applied it all, you would sail through the terrible teenage years without so much as finding a cigarette butt under your daughter's pillow. The testing child is unlikely to let you get away with this.

One mother, whose children are now in their

twenties, said this: 'It's true that our second child was difficult, but I think part of it was that he came into the world and saw that most of the good pitches were already taken. The "Academic Achievement" pitch was already taken by his older brother, as was the "Orderly Bedroom" along with "Helping Around the House". I think he felt there was little point trying to compete in those areas because he knew he just couldn't be *that* good. And so he decided to get a little attention (or perhaps for that read "significance") in other ways – like painting the cat pink when he was a toddler and being the class clown when he hit the teenage years.'

But whether your child is compliant or testing – or a mixture of each – try to remember that the teenage years are the time when they are developing in just about every way: physical, emotional and spiritual. This is a time for experimentation, for trying out what does and doesn't work.[1] The very bad news is that as parents, it means we are going to be on the sharp end of a lot of it. But the other thing to remember is that for most teenagers many of these experiences are *experiments* – not lifestyle choices.

The following pages contain three principles that many parents have found helpful with their testing teenager. Any one of these can revolutionise your relationship with your child but, even more important, will help to build a relationship that will last a lifetime.

Principle Number One: Take a second look

If they were asked what elements of a testing teenager's character they would like to change, most parents would say, 'How long have you got?' Our secret hope might be that they become more like our friend's compliant child or a compliant sibling. And this tends to be in the *areas that are most easily measured* – academic achievement, tidiness, organisational abilities. The great sadness is that in focusing on what can easily be measured, we may miss incredible talents they have in areas that are not so easily observed. We are so consumed with changing them – in getting them to fulfil some formula that looks like success to *us* – that we overlook other qualities. We may have a son whose bedroom constantly looks as though a small hurricane has hit it, whose school work is left undone, and whom we discover has started to smoke. We think 'Where did I go wrong?' So we devote all our energies into getting him to respect his clothes and hang them up properly, keep his room tidy and get coursework in on time, and into warning him of the foolishness of smoking. All these are reasonable aims, but they mean that the air is always filled with comments like: 'Your room is a mess!', 'If you don't finish that essay tonight, you're not going to the party on Saturday!' and 'You've been smoking again, haven't you?'

The only problem is that sometimes we miss the fact that he is a loyal friend; he has a large heart that cannot but reach out to those who are in need – we sometimes see him spend some of his pocket money to help the destitute – and he has a way of looking at life that is often surprisingly insightful.[2] And so, if we are wise, then alongside the comments about tidiness, smoking and coursework (which are all absolutely necessary) will be other ones that acknowledge different qualities: 'You are such a good friend,' 'I was proud of you when you helped that man who'd broken down,' 'You're good at this – what's your opinion?'

These are qualities that rarely get into school reports, but however we do it we must encourage these wonderful traits because when he is an adult, it is those we will value most.

The testing teenager

Some time ago I had lunch with a very successful businessman. As we chatted I asked him to tell me about his family. He said, 'I have three children. My oldest daughter is twenty-five – she's doing a PhD.' He went on to tell me about his second child – another daughter, aged twenty-three, who had just started her MA. At this juncture he stopped talking and started eating. After a short silence I asked, 'What about your third child?' He shrugged his shoulders and put his knife and fork down, 'Oh, he's nineteen and dyslexic. His bedroom's a mess, he doesn't do his college work, he gets parking tickets and forgets to pay them. I tell him, "You'd better sharpen up – it's a tough world out there!"'

I, too, put my knife and fork down and turned to face my lunch companion, 'Excuse my asking this, but can you remember ever praising your son for *anything*?'

He replied, 'I really can't.'

I said, 'When you go home tonight, find something he has done remotely well and praise him for it. It will revolutionise your relationship with him.'

To his credit he said he would.

In other words, sometimes with the testing child – *we have to take a second look.*

Principle Number Two: Keep them busy

The most basic reason it is vital to keep our children busy is not to use the teenage years to introduce them to the wonders of the arts or great literature, or even for them to become sporting stars, it is simply to make them so exhausted that they don't have the energy to get into trouble. The very last thing the testing teenager needs is a six-week school holiday,[3] where he or she is at home alone, with no idea what to do on day 1, never mind day 31. The same is true of evenings and weekends.

Before you start putting pen to paper and accuse me of encouraging you to control your teenagers so they won't have time for a social life, let me reassure you that this is the least of your worries – most of them won't let you do that anyway. It is simply a strategy to give you some extra help in getting your child through this turbulent period – especially the younger teenage years. Every hour, every evening, every summer holiday where they are involved in some structured leisure pursuit, is one less opportunity for them to drive you or somebody else crazy.[4]

If your child is sporty, then such activities are easier

to come by, but we dare not give up on this strategy even if our teenager couldn't score a goal to save his life. It doesn't have to be expensive, or involve you in a constant shuttle from Scouts, to karate, from piano to ballet. The main ingredients are structure. It needs to be an activity they enjoy and involves meeting others, a level of commitment and developing a skill. But before you rush out and buy that musical instrument, remember that it may not turn out exactly as you imagine. Your hope is to see Carl plucking away at a Spanish guitar as part of the National Youth Orchestra. What actually happens is that he gets together most nights of the week with three mates who manage to murder the finest heavy metal music ever written!

But there's another reason this is important – and it's not just about keeping them busy. It has to do with dignity. When we help our teenagers develop a skill, we give them a sense of self-worth that may well help them resist some of the more dangerous pressures to gain acceptance by their peers. Having a skill builds confidence, gives purpose and, in the case of a testing teenager who shares a home with a compliant sibling, may just save the day. The reason behind this is not hard to fathom. That testing teenage daughter lives all her life with the knowledge that in most of the categories of family life her compliant sibling scores As. She's not stupid; she knows her parents love her sister's sunny disposition and the way she's always asked to take the lead in school plays. She watches in despair as her sister helps around the house, cleans out the rabbit cage, and greets guests and makes them coffee. And all of this creates two opposing emotions in her. First, she sometimes thinks she hates her sister for being such a creep, but second, another part of her longs for the acceptance and praise that she senses her sister enjoys from her parents.

The only problem is that she believes there is nothing in her life that her sister can't do better than her. At least, that was true until she took up ice-hockey. Now she's at the rink at least three evenings a week; she can't remember how she had so much time to hang around every evening outside the local corner shop. Every weekend she's in a match. And the really cool thing is that she knows her parents are proud of her. They still have loads of rows in the house and her goody-two-shoes sister is still top of the pile in every other category – except for this. And when she scores a goal or even just makes a great pass, she senses her parents on the rink-side, smiling. And it makes her feel warm inside and kind of special.

Before we leave this topic, just take a moment to consider the testing teenager who, in addition to pushing the normal boundaries, also seems determined to risk life and limb at any opportunity. If somebody in their class is going to 'give it a go' you can be sure that your son or daughter will be one of them. They are easily bored, restless souls who are not so much looking for a chance to get into trouble, as a chance to get into *anything*. One of the most perplexing aspects of teenagers' lives for parents to understand is their son or daughter's willingness to take risks. Why, we ask, would he ride his skateboard off such a high wall? Doesn't she understand that climbing out of her bedroom window to meet the boyfriend we have banned her from seeing for a week may be romantic, but means she risks breaking her neck? Here again, some recent research into what's going on in the grey matter of the brain may help us understand.

The chemical dopamine is one of the key neurotransmitters in the brain. All adults need it to function normally, but excess levels of it in the teenage brain seem to play a central role in stimulating risky behaviour in some teenagers.[5] We can't shut it off, but what we might want to think about is the range of potential risk-taking possibilities available to our teenagers. If their environment only offers risk-taking around cars, drugs, alcohol or sex, then some teenagers are going to take risks with these. Offering them opportunities to take more controlled risks may be one of the best things a parent can do for them. Of course, every child is different but, for some, scaring the life out of them in something of a 'structured' environment – perhaps rock-climbing, canoeing, skate-boarding or even the adrenaline rush of performing on the first night of a play – may give them enough thrills without too many serious spills.

Over the last fifteen years I have been involved in running holidays for single parents and their children. They are based at outdoor activity centres and it is fascinating to watch how teenagers who, on the first day, look down their noses at the activities on offer, often change by the end of the week, not only in achievement and enjoyment, but in attitude.

Principle Number Three: Choose your battles

I wasn't a particularly strong child and my parents, like millions of others, were no doubt worried about my being bullied. My father's response to this was to buy two sets of boxing gloves and three times a week, in our tiny living room, to teach me to fight. It didn't go well for many reasons. First, my father was rather short of boxing skills himself and the dreadful combination of this with my awkwardness often led to him pulling the gloves off and mumbling, 'You couldn't box eggs!' My mother had a different strategy to impart to me. She would occasionally recite a little rhyme to me: 'He who fights and runs away, lives to fight another day.'

Over the years, and especially as the father of teenagers, it is my mother's strategy I have most warmed to – and I think military history is on her side. It is true that Custer's last stand was brave, heroic and magnificent, but it was his *last* stand. In contrast, the Allies' retreat from Dunkirk seemed humiliating at the time, but turned out to be a triumph. They were fatigued, outnumbered and ill-equipped, and simply decided it was not a battle they wanted to fight. The key to winning wars is not to plan for last stands. And when we do pick a battle, it's best to make sure we're in a reasonable condition to fight it – it may not be best to pick a fight with our teenager last thing at night after a bad day at work and when we've got a migraine coming on.

If you have a testing teenager you will find that the opportunities for last stands are many. They begin with his appearance when he goes to school and then what he says when he comes home. They move on to how quickly he starts his homework, what of his meal he leaves untouched and whether he helps with the washing-up. The fight then intensifies as to how long he stays on the phone to his friends and what time he goes out/comes in/gets up the next day. And in all of this we have not even touched on pierced noses, loud music, long faces and a hamster so neglected he can't even be bothered to get on his wheel.

If we choose to fight every battle, our homes will be filled with the sounds of warfare and our teenagers will believe that we are always on their backs; but there is a much deeper problem even than that. When my daughter was small she used to have a little device she used when she knew she was going to be told off. She would put her hands over her ears and yell, 'I can't hear you! I can't hear you!' If we fight *every* battle, our teenagers will never discover the ones that really do matter to us.

This is a particular danger for parents who are shooting for perfection: they want their teenagers to reach and maintain the highest standards in every area of their lives. It sounds laudable, but has terrible dangers inherent in it. Imagine their teenage son is walking a high-wire. It's dangerous; the teenager occasionally wobbles, but looks as though he might make it to the end. The only problem is that underneath the wire his mother is shouting, 'Your shirt's hanging out!', 'Your hair is too long!', 'Why don't you smile more?' It seems these parents just cannot help themselves. But they need to know that so often they make it harder, not easier, for the teenager who is already struggling to make it to the other side. One father said, 'These days I try to say yes to everything I possibly can, but that means I fight the "no"s tooth and nail.'

I'm sure he's right. Some battles are not only worth fighting, they are absolutely vital. In spite of what I've just said above, the saddest teenagers on the face of the earth are not those whose parents are always nagging – awful though that is – it is those who have come to believe that their parents don't care what they do. The children of such parents may have an easy time of it in the area of discipline, but the lack of boundaries reinforced by love leads to tremendous insecurity. And this causes huge problems. I think of a young girl sleeping rough who said, 'I used to moan that my parents wanted me in at a certain time every night. I wish somebody cared what time I came home now.'

I talked with a psychologist recently who was himself a parent. He said, 'The problem is that many parents don't really love their kids.' I was a little surprised, to say the least. I think I can say I have never met a parent, no matter how wrong they had got their parenting, whom I thought did *not* love their children. He went on, 'They think they love their children. They provide for them. They are glad when they do well. But what really gives them away is that they are so insecure in that love. They want to be their child's best friend, but the problem is that parents who really love their children have to do things that best friends don't. They have to set boundaries and enforce them. They have to say no. They have to be willing to be unpopular for a while.

What matters is not that I am my teenager's mate – he's got lots of those – but that I am his father. And that he knows that even when I have a go at him over something, I still love him.'

So we all have to decide which are the important battles – and they will be different for each of us. We need consistency here, both in terms of parents backing each other up and in terms of what matters – not 'insignificant' one day and 'a big issue' the next. One father told me that for him, the choice of battle was the issue of what time his teenager came in at night.[6] He said he had dreaded the day when his son hit the teenage years because he knew that with his son's testing personality they would have conflict over the issue of curfews. He decided to try a strategy that combined praise, picking your battles and tough discipline. His son is now an adult, but looking back the father told me that he thought it had worked. They'd had plenty of ongoing fights – and his son tested them in many ways – but on the big battleground of curfews he thought it was fair to say that everybody, including his son, felt a winner. Listen to him tell his story in his own words.

The time that I'd been dreading came. Lee was about fourteen and said, 'Dad, I'm going out tonight with my friends and I want to stay out later than usual.' His normal time to be in was at 9.30pm.

'OK,' I said. 'You can come in at 10pm.'

He looked a little shocked that I had agreed so easily and said, 'Thanks, Dad!'

I replied, '10pm, mind you. On the dot.'

'OK, Dad.'

He came in at five minutes past ten. I went bananas. In fact I went more bananas than I felt – it's a little easier when you're acting. 'We had an agreement that you'd come in at ten and you've broken your part of it.'

'Dad,' he said, 'it's just five minutes.'

I said, 'I want to be as generous to you as I can be in all of this, but to do that we have to work together. Whatever time we say – that's it. On the dot!'

He mumbled and grumbled, but the next three times he came in bang on time. On the fourth time he rang to say that a friend's father was delayed in picking them up and I accepted that.

On the fifth occasion my son asked if he could

stay out until 10.15pm as there was something special on.

I said, 'No, you can stay out until 10.30pm.'

He looked at me as though he was sure I really had lost it, so I explained: 'I can trust you. You always come in on time now.'

That father told me that all through his son's teenage years they had plenty of hassles but curfews weren't part of them.

It may help us to choose the right battles if we realise that for teenagers these are the years of experiments[7] – both good and bad ones. We cut toddlers a lot more slack in this area than teenagers. When our three-year-old tries to put his finger in the electric socket we don't say, 'Oh dear, I wonder if he's going to spend the rest of his life putting his finger in electric sockets?' The truth is that there seems to be something in the human psyche that is hard-wired to touch the plate when the waiter warns, 'Be careful – it's hot.' Of course, the experimentation of the teenage years holds more potential for harm. Nevertheless, the parent whose fear causes him to over-protect his teenager may send her into adult life in even greater danger.

But what if it all goes wrong? You've had a good relationship with your teenager. You've always let him know he is loved unconditionally, at the same time as setting clear boundaries. And yet it is in your son's bedroom that you have found the drugs. It was psychologist Dr John White who said, 'There is no pain like parental pain.'[8] I believe it. But I also believe, 'There is no guilt like parental guilt.' We have to realise that irrespective of how good a job we have made of parenting, the time comes for our children when they make their own choices – and sometimes they are bad ones. And if our worst fears are realised, then perhaps the first thing to do is to lay aside false guilt. It tends to paralyse us. It gets us so caught up with our feelings of parental responsibility that we are not able to think clearly about the right parental *response* – in other words, what to actually do about the situation.

And before we leave the issue of the testing teenager, I want to say just a word for parents who happen to be reading while their children are still small. I know it's difficult when your toddler is stamping and kicking in the supermarket because she wants a bag of sweets. She may be threatening to embarrass you by throwing cartons of yoghurt over the other shoppers unless she gets her way. But if you do choose to fight that battle, then even if a dozen customers go home covered from head to foot in 'Muller Light', make sure you win it. The reason is clear: although it's hard at the time, it doesn't come near, not *near*, to having a fourteen-year-old girl looking you in the eye and saying 'No.'

Build up all the 'awe' you can when they are small . . . you're going to need it.

Since my 16-year-old son recently received a pay-as-you-go mobile phone as a gift, I've asked him to use it to call home if he's out past his curfew. One Saturday night while waiting up for him, I dozed off in front of the TV. Later I woke to realise that there was no sign of him, and there had been no call.

Irate, I punched in his number. When he answered, I demanded, 'Where are you, and why haven't you bothered to call?'

'Dad,' he sleepily replied, 'I'm upstairs in bed. I've been home for an hour.'

4

School

There is an incredible line in Willy Russell's play *Blood Brothers*. An adult is looking at a group of small children at play and says, 'And who'd dare tell the lambs in spring, what fate the later seasons bring.' Whenever I pass an infants' school playground I sometimes think of those words. For many children, Years 1 to 6 are reasonably enjoyable, but for some the journey to secondary school at age eleven is a traumatic one, which brings fresh and often difficult challenges for both the children and their parents.

In this new arena even children who have been reasonably confident socially, and felt adequate in academic subjects, can suddenly lose their nerve. The teachers may seem totally focused on achievement[1] (and who can blame them with yet another target looming up?). Children in this new school may be banded according to ability and find themselves constantly asking themselves, 'Am I good enough?' But it's not just academic pressure they face. At a time in their lives when they are at their most vulnerable, they suddenly have to negotiate a whole new set of relationships. And there may be some shocks: a child who had a best friend in the junior school may suddenly find herself standing alone in the playground as her former soul-mate finds new and more exciting company.

I'm pretty sure that most adults have no real idea of what school is like today for some teenagers. One boy said to me, 'When I get home from school my parents say to me, "What did you do today?" And I say, "Nothing." And then they say, "Well, you must have done *something*!" and I say, "Well . . . stuff." And they say, "What stuff?" ' He sighed and said, 'Sometimes I'd like to tell them the truth and say, "Actually, I've spent most of the day fighting. I've been fighting teachers who are on my back trying to get me to learn things I, and they, know I will never use again. I've been fighting to stay part of my group of friends because somebody said I told a teacher that a kid had been smoking – believe me, I wouldn't have told if the kid had been on fire. And finally, I've spent the day fighting – or rather, hiding from – a kid in Year 10 who said he's going to kill me. How's that for a day? And you know what? That's most days."'

But what can a parent do to help? Over the years I've had countless conversations with parents who have shared with me their number one tip for getting a teenager through the school years. I've often thought to myself, 'I wish I'd heard that when my kids were ten, not twenty!' The problem with being a parent is that just about the time you get the hang of it, you're redundant. (That is just as true for those who write books on the stuff as the rest!) From all those tips, I've selected just three. I wish I'd learnt every one of them a whole lot earlier!

Tip Number One: The most important A-star is emotional health

A school report that shows their child is doing well academically can so easily be seen by parents as the ultimate sign that all is well. But teenage 'wellness' is deeper than that. Patrick West and Helen Sweeting of

Glasgow University have released the results of a study that ought to be a check to every mother or father whose only waking thought is the number of A-stars their offspring will achieve. They discovered a huge leap in the rates of emotional disturbance among high-achieving girls. 'Compared with girls just sixteen years ago, young girls are now dramatically – and worryingly – more miserable.'[2]

And if that's all it is – a bit of misery for the sake of some good grades – it would probably be worthwhile, but it isn't. In middle-class teenage girls, serious mental illness – the kind that can require hospitalisation – has risen threefold. Mary Macleod, Chief Executive of the National Family and Parenting Institute, said that the pressure with regard to examination results is at such a pitch that some girls will find the stress too much and attempt to kill themselves.[3]

If we have any doubt as to the extent of the pressure, then perhaps listening to the chilling words of seventeen-year-old Jessica Wear may convince us: 'The school put me under so much pressure. They used to say to me, "We've only had one B in the last five years – *don't be the second*." '[4]

The problem for some parents in this area is not that their child won't try hard enough in examinations, it is that they will be consumed by the need to reach perfection. They will be plagued by the prospect of failure and just as the anorexic complains that they are fat even while looking emaciated, so this child will feel a total failure for dropping just a few marks along the way.

The great sadness is that such a child doesn't even enjoy her (and this problem is much greater among girls) successes. Even as she receives an accolade from the teacher for another wonderful result, a small but insistent voice will whisper to her, 'Can you be that good next time? Can you go on being top?' Charlotte put it like this: 'If I do something less than perfectly I will think about it for a long time. It's petty, but in my mock GCSEs I got two As and A-stars in the rest. One of the As [i.e. not an A-star] was in Maths and I cried for so long. It was my best subject and I didn't get the top grade. Why not?'[5]

Anthony Seldon, Master of Wellington College, commented on the fact that one Harley Street psychiatrist is seeing five children from the same class of one hothouse London school: 'They are suffering from depression, anorexia, and a sense of worthlessness brought on by the feeling that they're trying to fulfil the goals of others rather than their own. The obsession with exams is wrong; most reasonable people accept this truth, but barely anything is being done about it.'[6]

Psychologist Madeline Levine talks of teenagers who have become paranoid about pleasing their parents. This is to the extent that a fourteen-year-old boy told her he is considering hacking into his school's computer system in order to raise his Maths grade and an academically outstanding pupil thinks of suicide when her SAT scores come back marginally lower than she has expected. Levine says: 'We need to examine our parenting paradigm. Raising children has come to look more and more like a business endeavour and less and less like an endeavour of the heart. We are overly concerned with "the bottom line", with how our children "do" rather than who our children "are".'[7]

On realising what was happening in his daughter's life, one father who had achieved a high measure of success in his professional life actually came to see that sometimes the cost to children of constantly trying to achieve can simply be too great. He said, 'My daughter used to be bright, lively and full of laughter, but she has become anxious, withdrawn and totally consumed with her grades. I often catch her crying. I want her to think not just about physics and chemistry, but about going out with her friends on a Saturday night. Of course I want her to do well – but not at this price.'

Before we leave the issue of academic achievements it may be worth saying that with some children, especially in the later teenage years, the battle in this area can become so fierce that it risks destroying our relationship with them. Whether our problem with our child is, as one mother put it, 'rust out' rather than 'burn out', whether our teenager is trying very hard, but simply can't keep up, or whether our perfectionist daughter is in danger of crashing emotionally, the truth is that there are things going on in the teenage years that are even more important than passing exams: issues of relationships, a sense of self-worth, and the formulation of ideas as to what works in life and what doesn't.[8] They can take an A-level in Geography when they are thirty, but when some boy breaks their heart at seventeen, or the panic attacks are getting worse, a cup of coffee with the mother or father they still have a relationship with can't be postponed.

Tip Number Two: Don't read their school reports as though they are a prophecy of their future lives

One of the greatest tests that parents of teenagers have to face is that of trying to help our children achieve their potential in the academic arena. And it's right that this particular battle should matter to us: young people who leave school with some decent qualifications have more choices available to them in later life. With some children this part, at least, will be a walk in the park – they are keen to learn and would memorise the telephone directory if there was an examination on it. But with other children we had better expect the academic battle to be both bloody and protracted, for it is here that the long-term view of the parent (university, career path, marriage, children, comfortable retirement) and the short-term view of the teenager (watching *Neighbours*, going out with Jake tonight, and selling his iPod on eBay) come into sharpest conflict.

And the jury is out on whether it's all worth it. On the one hand, you have young men and women in their twenties with good degrees and great jobs who say, 'If my father hadn't locked me in my bedroom to learn the kings and queens of England I'd never have passed GCSE History. I gave him a hard time, but I'm so glad he did it.' On the other hand, we meet a disheartened mother who's given the task of motivating her teenager her very best shot. She's bought study guides that still remain in their wrappers, and got an evening job to pay for tutors who tried to break the news to her that her offspring was not really interested in learning French irregular verbs. She's attended parent–teacher evenings where she's discussed strategies to lift her son's performance and begged teachers to keep their voices down. But none of it seems to have made much difference.

So what do we do? The truth is we have to give it our best shot; a mother or father's input can make an incredible difference in this area.[9] But here is where it gets tricky and gives a good example of why parenting really is the toughest job on the face of the earth. (President Theodore Roosevelt said, 'I can be president of the United States or I can control Alice [his daughter]. I cannot possibly do both.') On the one hand, we may be scared of pushing our children too hard – or even worse, giving them the impression that all we care about is their grades. On the other hand we can be fearful that we are going too easy on them and abdicating our responsibility for getting a child who is talented but basically lazy off his bottom. And the truth is we have to make a judgement about our particular child. Most parents are fairly accurate judges of their children's potential. They know full well that one child is trying as hard as possible but is just not able to lift her grades, while another says that school is boring and finds any excuse for not doing his homework, not because he is incapable of it, but because he just isn't making the necessary effort. So, in the latter case, the parents may well insist that their child puts in an hour's piano practice for a forthcoming exam before letting him go to football training and may decide not to allow him to go out with his mates until he has plumbed the depths of that day's science project. It's true that these decisions probably don't endear them to their teenager, but sometimes taking a hit in the popularity stakes is what parenting is about. Often it's worth sinking a little in the 'Best Father in Brighton' ratings, so that we can at least see whether, under all that lethargy, there is a budding scientist who just needs a bit of a prod to get going.

And incidentally, it's vital that parents present a united front on this issue.

But in the midst of all this coursework warfare, and even if all our efforts seem to have failed and the reports come home with depressingly similar comments (there are times when you don't want to know that Jack is 'lively and cheerful' in class – you'd settle once in a while for 'boring and miserable' if it came with some better grades), we should remember a principle so vital it should be put on a fridge magnet the size of a dustbin lid: *Don't read the score at half time.*

School reports catalogue achievements at a certain stage of a person's life in a narrow band of subjects, covering information much of which the child will never use again during the rest of his life. They also tend to favour children who have an academic bent as opposed to a practical one. This may be a little short-sighted. If we approached many adults today and asked them if they would like to swap their A-levels and degree for a qualification in plumbing or bricklaying, we'd get killed in the rush. And we need to remember the things that reports *don't* measure, such as 'savvy' – that intrinsic ability some people have to make a success of life by using their native wit. I think of a boy of eight who came home from school and said to his father, 'Dad, the teachers and kids in my school are crazy.'

'Why's that, Son?'

'Because they're all in there trying to learn their nine times table.'

'What's wrong with that?'

'We've all got calculators on our mobile phones, Dad.'

'Well, Son, someday you might be somewhere without your mobile phone and need to know what nine nines are.'

'If I am, I'll ask the kid next to me who learnt them.'

I'm not saying this boy's attitude was entirely right, but I do believe he has a way of looking at life that may just see him through – though it doesn't have a chance of ever getting on a school report.

And anyway, even if your child seems totally disinterested in passing exams at the moment, the day may come when he finds something in life he really wants to do. And if Biology GCSE is a gateway to it, you may well find him reciting the blood circulation system of the African desert frog in his sleep.

School

I wasn't very good at school. My home background wasn't an academic one and the grammar school in which I somehow ended up may as well as have been Mars. I didn't understand how to study, how to pass exams or even the importance of the simple things (such as, if there are three questions on the examination paper and you answer the first two so brilliantly that you don't have time to do the last one, then your chances of getting a good grade are low). My parents tried to help as much as possible, but to be honest it was another world to them as well. I still have the school report I took home at the end of the Easter term when I was fourteen. In it my form master had written: 'He is making no use of what little ability he has.'

My friend in school was Steve. He was no better than I was at passing exams. In his case it was not our form master, but a language teacher who yelled at him, 'You're going to be a failure.' Some years ago I was lecturing at a university to a group of solicitors and during a coffee break I ambled along the corridors of the law faculty. I was interested to find out whether or not a rumour I'd heard about Steve was true. I passed the doors of lecturers and senior lecturers, and

71

then came to one marked 'Professor'. I knocked. When I went in, Steve had his feet on the desk just as he used to in the Maths class.

'Robert Parsons!' he yelled. I smiled at him: 'Hello, Failure.'

Tip Number Three: Help your teenager discover his strengths

Dewi Williams, my English teacher, changed my life. When he read *Under Milk Wood* I felt as if Dylan Thomas himself was in my classroom. And while the rest of the teachers were having sleepless nights about my obvious lack of talent in Chemistry, Physics and Maths, all Dewi cared about was how I could write better essays. He couldn't help himself; he was in love with literature.

Perhaps he should have been different with me. Perhaps other teachers said to him in the staff-room, 'Why don't you get that boy to care a bit more about quadratic equations and less about literature?' But if they did say it, he didn't listen. All he wanted to do was make me even better at the one thing in school I was good at. While my books in other subjects were filled with crosses, underlinings and 'See me!', my English books had ticks next to paragraphs and comments such as, 'I like this!', 'This is very good' and on one occasion, 'Let's try to get this into print!' And then a strange thing began to happen. As, through the years, my confidence in that single area grew, I began to believe that I could achieve things elsewhere. Dewi was the greatest teacher I have ever known. He knew all along he wasn't just teaching me English. He was giving me an education – in myself.

We can emulate him as parents. Imagine the scene: our teenage daughter comes home with her school report. She's got an A in History, a B in Maths and a D in French. What do we spend most of the next hour talking about? The French of course! We say, 'How can we help you do better in your French? Shall we get you some study guides in GCSE French? How about some audio tapes or perhaps a tutor?'

Where's the parent who will say, 'Let's get you a tutor for your History!'

'But, Mum, I got an A in History!'

'I know. Let's make you even better at what you're good at.'

I understand the need to get a spread of GCSEs –

and the pressure therefore of trying to keep all the plates in the air – but especially with the seemingly less able child, it's vital to send them into life knowing that they have found at least one strength and that they have a parent who is helping them to develop it. The whole world wants to work on my weaknesses, but I agree with Donald Clifton and Paula Nelson, authors of *Soar with Your Strengths*, who said, 'If you want to be successful, find out what you don't do well and stop doing it.'[10]

If we are to be successful as parents of teenagers then of course we have to work in tandem with their schools to help achieve some measure of academic success. But we have an even more important task than that. It is to do what teachers often cannot do because of time restrictions, curriculum demands or sheer size of classes: it is to bring another way of looking at life that will give our teenagers a sense of perspective, and for many who are struggling – a sense of hope.

5

Bullying

Somewhere this morning a child woke with a dreadful fear in his gut. He pulled the duvet around him and lay thinking about the day ahead. His mother shouted upstairs that he was running late for school. He finally hauled himself out of bed – and then suddenly got straight back in. When his mother came into the room she was all set to drag him out of bed if necessary, but then she saw him lying with his head buried in the pillow. She could hear the dreadful gasps of uncontrollable crying and see his body shaking beneath the duvet. 'What on earth is the matter?' she said. It took several efforts to get him to speak, but finally he said, 'I'm not well. My stomach is hurting again. I can't go to school today.'

Bullying, although often carried on in secret,

permeates every aspect of a child's life. It reaches into their social life, touches their relationships and can destroy their self-esteem. It can lead to them becoming aggressive, depressed, and even to considering suicide. But often the effects of bullying reach much further than the obvious victim. More than half of male bullies and a quarter of girl bullies said they had been threatened with physical violence at school themselves. Girls who are bullies are more than three times as likely as non-bullies to have tried drugs while looking for 'a release from tension and depression', and boys who are bullies are twice as likely as non-bullies to have been in trouble with the police. Bullies are six times more likely to have a criminal record by the age of twenty-four.[1]

The children's charity ChildLine recently announced a 42 per cent increase in the number of children counselled by the charity about bullying and said this single issue now accounts for one in four calls it receives – over thirty-one thousand in the past year.[2] The chances of your child being bullied or being involved in bullying are high.[3] And before you dash a letter off to me protesting, remember that those who simply do nothing and join in the laughter are, in the victims' eyes, part of the problem. Even so, don't be too hard on your child. One fifteen-year-old said, 'In our school you don't have a choice: you either join in with the bullying of the losers or you become one.'

The cruelty of the young is almost without parallel in later life. This is not because, as adults, we do not do worse things to each other, but because the cruelties of the playground are practised on those who, at more than any other time of their lives, want to be accepted by their peers. Emily is fourteen. She said, 'When I was little, in primary school we sometimes used to bully each other, but it didn't feel that bad. One day some girls said that I had a deadly disease and that if anyone touched me they would get it. I just rushed around the playground touching everybody! But now I am fourteen and it's much worse. The same group of girls taunts me most days. They don't hit me or anything, they just call me names like "slag" or "moron". Sometimes I just go into the toilets and be sick. Sometimes I would like to kill myself.'

Bullying takes many forms. It includes teasing, name calling[4] and being left out – as happened to Mark, aged thirteen, when one of his friends rang everybody else and they all decided not to go to his birthday party. He was left having a paint-ball expedition with him, his father and a distant uncle. Bullying could be being pushed, hit, threatened or having possessions hidden. It may involve rumours about the child or his family or abuse because of race, disability or sexuality.

And cyberspace is providing a brand new arena for the bullies. In a recent survey, one in ten teenagers interviewed said they had received threatening emails or text messages, and more than a quarter said somebody had published misleading information about them on the web.[5] Commenting on the survey, Elaine Peace of the children's charity NCH put it like this: 'As technology has become more sophisticated, so has the way children are being bullied.'[6]

Experts have seen a range of bullying, from abusive emails to manipulation of photographs of the victim. Imagine being fourteen years old and conscious of your slightly protruding ears. One day a friend suggests you have a look at your photograph on a web page. When you log on you see that somebody has put an elephant's ears onto your head.

So bullying may take many forms, but whatever it involves, one thing is certain: it ruins children's lives. It affects their physical and mental health, damages their capacity for learning and, for a minority, affects forever the way they interact with peers and colleagues. A friend of mine who has spent years as a counsellor told me that conversations she'd had with teenagers who were being bullied were among the most distressing she has ever experienced.

This is how one girl described her experience of being bullied via her mobile phone and computer:

One time I kept getting calls, I was really scared. I phoned my friend and she wasn't at home so I couldn't talk to her. Then I started getting emails and texts at school and they were still saying horrible stuff. It made me feel so scared that I couldn't go home alone. I'd be too scared to walk because they kept saying they knew where I lived and they were watching me all the time. Every time I went near somebody I didn't know I'd be scared and I would have to stand near somebody else. Gradually they started to leave me alone, the calls started to die down and so did the texts but I was still scared for a few weeks after. Some people have nasty minds and they don't care about anyone but themselves, even if they're really badly hurting someone, they just want to feel really big and tough.[1]

Of course, for the teenager in this situation the big questions are: 'Who do you tell?' and perhaps even harder to answer, '*How* do you tell?' Telling is always right and yet for many children the risks inherent in exposing the bullies are just too great to take. If you tell teachers, they might go straight to the bully and that will just make things worse. If you tell friends, they might tell somebody else. If you tell your parents, they might 'go straight up to the school'. That's exactly what happened to Vicky. She had been putting up with people calling her a 'tart' and hiding her books, but when her best friend joined in, Vicky told her mum all about it. This is how Vicky described what happened next: 'My mum went potty. She got straight on the phone to the Head and told him he had better sort it. He did. The name calling stopped and now nobody hides my books. The only problem is, nobody talks to me either. I know my mum thought she was doing right, but she's just made it all ten times worse. I wish I'd never told her.'

Vicky's mum may have got it wrong on that occasion, but time and time again when asked, 'Who would you prefer to talk to about the bullying?' teenagers say, 'My parents.' Again, this is both good and bad news. It's good to know we are the ones they want to confide in, but bad because so often we just aren't sure how to handle it.

I want to share some specific strategies to help our teenagers deal with bullying, but first there is something that is top of the agenda in helping children who are experiencing *any* trauma. It is *listening*. This is how sixteen-year-old Marianne put it:

At first I just wanted to talk about how I was feeling. I needed to know that I was not a bad person because of what was happening. I needed to know that there was no shame in my mum's eyes. I needed to know that she loved me. I wanted to cry with her sitting by me. I didn't expect her to solve the bullying – in fact I knew it wouldn't be that simple. When we first spoke, I didn't want to hear her ideas about what we were going to do. I needed her to focus on my feelings. It was just a relief to talk and to get the feelings off my chest. My mum listened to me and I felt like I mattered and I had some hope.

So what *can* a parent do?

• The first thing is a 'don't'. Don't take over. It was hard enough for your child to talk to you about it and now it's important that they feel a measure of control in how it's going to be dealt with. Some good lines to avoid are:

  'Right! I'm going straight down to the school.'
  'Just ignore them.'
  'What you should do is . . .'
  'OK! That does it! I'm taking you straight out of that school!'
  'Just stand up to them. Bullies hate that!'

Simon decided to tell his youth worker he was being bullied. The youth worker asked him if he'd told anybody about it. Simon hesitated, 'I told my dad, but he just told me to knock their block off – and if I did, he'd support me.' Simon dropped his head and went on, 'The only thing is, I'm not that type.'

Bullying

The youth worker asked, 'So who else have you told about the bullying?'

Simon said, 'Oh – nobody. What's the point?'

- Praise your child for telling you about the situation. Tell them you realise how hard it must have been for them to tell somebody and how pleased you are that they have chosen you. This is not just a nice idea. Many children who have been bullied experience 'double shame' – not just their own for being bullied, but the shame of hurting a parent in the telling of it.

- Ask them what they think might be a way ahead; brainstorm some options with them; convince them that they have some control and ownership of the outcome. Remember that your teenager may not be an expert on bullying, but they are the expert on *their* school and the bullies in it. If possible, avoid the 'victim' label; this can carry a sense of inevitability with it.

- Every school should have a bullying policy and it's worth finding out about the one at your child's school. If you and your teenager agree that the issue needs to be taken to the school, ask them how they want to go about it and which teacher they would like to talk to first. Some schools have a 'Peer Support' system whereby selected older pupils are trained to be confidential listeners and supporters for younger pupils. If you do talk to the school, it's a good idea to make a note of what they say they are going to do.

- Don't be upset if your teenager wants to talk to other adults or friends about the problem. The truth is, they need all the help they can get and so do you! Talk to friends about it – preferably friends who don't have children at the same school. If the bullying is hard to prove and is ongoing, you may suggest your child keeps a diary of the incidents. You can download one from ChildLine's website.[8]

- Remember that, for your child, the bullying may be all-consuming. This may be a good time to ease up on the pressure in some less important areas – that untidy bedroom, for example – and to make sure that although life in school is hard, there are some good times outside of it. And above all, tell them that you love them, that they can always talk to you about it, and that you will come through this experience together.

When your child is older and this horrendous experience is just a memory, it may be that the way you dealt with it will earn you that ultimate accolade of parenting that kids sometimes award to parents when they themselves become adults. It is not presented to the mother or father who always got it right, were the coolest parents in the street, or were brilliant in dealing with impossible situations. No, it is given rather to those parents of whom a child can say: 'They were always there for me.'

6

Sex

In this dangerous world there are many lessons that parents have to get across to their children. We have to teach them how to cross the road, warn them that not every stranger who speaks to them kindly or offers them sweets has their good at heart, and tell them it's not always wise to pat dogs – especially on hot days. And all that without even mentioning cigarettes, hot stoves, swimming pools, stairs, irons and electric fans. The truth is that from the moment the umbilical cord is cut and the midwife hands us that bundle of flesh, we seem to be warning our child about danger.

So how can we explain the following? In a country that has the highest teenage pregnancy rate in Western Europe, in which the rates of infection by sexually transmitted diseases are climbing, and in which almost a third of young people have experienced sex before they are sixteen, why have so many parents decided not to talk to their children about sex?

I believe part of the answer lies in the changing nature of society. Take another glance at that list of potential hazards I mentioned a moment ago. Imagine you were a negligent parent and you warned your children of the dangers of *none of them*. You said absolutely nothing about irons that burn, stoves that scald, cars that maim, dogs that bite, cigarettes that kill, and electric fans that would take your fingers off as soon as look at you. What would be the outcome for your child? The short answer is that he may well still be alright. And the reason for this is that the rest of society – schools, magazines, television – are probably giving the same message you would have given them anyway.

The problem is that in the modern world, doing nothing won't work for sex. Parents can't rely on the rest of society to reinforce the messages they would want to pass on to their children. A former chief editor of a leading teenage magazine said this:

> *Parents are actually the most influential factors in teens' decisions about sex. Teens want to hear from their parents about sex and they need to. They have so much information coming at them from the media, friends and the Internet – the problem is they aren't getting the right information from the right places.*

And then she adds this sobering comment: 'The conversations with parents are *just not keeping up*.'[1] In other words, she is saying, 'Wake up and smell the coffee! Times have changed.'

One fifteen-year-old commented: 'Even when you're young, you are bombarded by people having sex. And it's used to sell us anything from Snickers to knickers.[2] We're told not to have under-age sex and yet you go to watch a fifteen-rated film and it's full of sex. You'd have to be frigid not to be affected.' Dr Samantha Callan, a social anthropologist, put it like this:

> *In such a world, any parent would be crazy if they abdicated the sexual education of their teenagers to others. That is not to say that schools, charitable organisations, faith groups, or government*

campaigns cannot play a part – but parents are key.

Professor David Paton talks of two key factors that could help reduce the rate of teenage pregnancies. The first is reducing poverty: a young woman who is poor and ill-educated with little prospect of good employment has little incentive to delay motherhood. And the second is healthy relationships within the family – *'whether parents are able to talk openly with their children'*.[3] The Government's Social Exclusion Unit Report has concluded that our teenage pregnancy rates will only come down if ordinary mums and dads are enlisted in the cause.[4]

The problem is that so many of us 'ordinary mums and dads' find it hard to talk to our teenagers about sex. We may feel wary in case it's all too much too soon. We are concerned that we might be planting an idea in their minds that wasn't there already – perhaps because when we were their age, having sex was high on the list of 'most unlikely things to happen this year'. On the other hand, we may believe they know it all anyway. We'd be wrong; many teenagers, for example, believe that condoms are 100 per cent effective against the possibility of pregnancy or the transmission of sexually transmitted diseases. But ignorance can be much more basic. The Kinsey Institute, America's famous sex research facility, is inundated every year by letters from teenagers who are desperate to know the truth about sex and sexuality but too embarrassed to talk to anybody about it. Here are some of the questions that appear regularly:

1 Can a girl get pregnant the first time she has sex?
2 Can a girl get pregnant during her period?
3 Can a girl get pregnant before starting her periods?
4 Can a girl get pregnant if she has sex standing up?
5 Can a girl get pregnant if her boyfriend withdraws his penis before he comes?
6 Can a girl get pregnant if she has sex in water?

The answer to all of these questions is yes – but you could be forgiven for wondering whether the teenagers who asked them were hoping for a no.

Or perhaps we feel we don't know enough; and we may well be right. One expert put it like this, 'There are many parents who have been copulating quite successfully for years, who couldn't answer the most basic questions asked by their children about sex.' The obvious question then to ask the expert is: 'If we've managed to get by with such a knowledge deficit, why can't we just pass on the little we know?' The simple answer is that the questions have changed. A generation ago we might have expected to pass the sex exam having revised the answer to, 'Mum, where do babies come from?' Today the opener may be, 'Hey, Dad, what exactly is oral sex?' One father I spoke to recently told me that for at least ten years after he was married he thought that oral sex meant talking about it.

But this is about much more than the mechanics of sex. We owe our teenagers the responsibility of knowing as much about sex as the writers in the teenage magazines they are reading and the friends in their class. In this most intimate of areas, they have a right to know what we believe and, as important, *why we believe it*.

We may not want to talk about it – perhaps we are embarrassed[5] – but the truth is that our children have a right to look to their parents for help in trying to bridge the gap between the sex of the glossies and real life.

Reasons to talk to your teenager about sex

- They are going to learn about sex whether you tell them or not. One teenager wrote his parents a letter in which he told them why he felt they had failed him. Perhaps it was unfair, but part of it read, 'I learned about sex from the street. Believe me – it wasn't a good place to learn it.'

- You may prevent some regrets. The problem is that although a teenager's body is old enough for sex, their emotions often aren't. Although about a third of girls are sexually active before they are sixteen, most of them say that with hindsight they wish they had waited.[6] The impression teenagers sometimes get is that everybody of their age is having sex.[7] Knowing that's not the case lifts the pressure to lose their virginity just to prove they are normal. It may be that in the heat of the moment they will remember a phrase they used to hear you say all the time: 'It's OK to just say no.'

- You get the chance to rehearse situations that are much more difficult 'live' (perhaps even when they might be under the influence of alcohol), such as how a girl should respond if a boy says, 'If you really loved me, you'd do it,' or reminding a boy that if somebody says no, they mean no.

They need your input to give them a fighting chance of balancing the myriad views about sex they hear elsewhere. *The Parentalk Guide to Your Child and Sex* puts it like this: 'If you're not influencing your child's thinking about sex and sexuality then you're about the only person in their life who isn't.'[8] Dr Samantha Callan says, 'Teenagers aren't fools: they know that sex is not just a trip down the skateboarding alley, but often it's only their parents who really reinforce the values they already hold, albeit tentatively, and which they want to have confirmed.'

Talking about sex

- Forget the 'big talk'. A better way is 'little by little'. It could be a discussion sparked by something that's happened to a friend, a piece of television news or even the soaps! One of the most effective pieces of education on sex I have ever seen occurred during a showing of *Friends*. Rachel tells Ross she is pregnant; he is utterly shocked. In fact, he is so shocked he says nothing for almost thirty seconds. Then he blurts out, 'But we used a condom!' Rachel explains that condoms don't always work. Ross looks even more shocked and screams out, 'They should say that on the box!'

- Try to talk about sex without embarrassment. You want your teenagers to have a positive view of sex and if possible a healthy future sex life. Sensing that their parents are embarrassed to talk about it makes sex seem tacky. Our daughters shouldn't be ashamed of their first period or our sons embarrassed by their first wet dream. Above all they need honest and straightforward explanations and advice. And sex shouldn't find a place first in their minds as something smutty.

- Remember we are aiming for a conversation not a diatribe. Sometimes, especially if we are angry or worried – perhaps when they are going out on a date – we feel the need to blurt it all out in one go. We're practically yelling advice at them as they walk hand in hand away from the house!

- Don't worry if they seem not to be listening; this is an important subject to them and you'll almost certainly have more of their attention than it seems. And again, as in other areas, we have to take the opportunity whenever it occurs – teenagers sometimes don't have the skill of linking the importance of the subject to the convenience of the time.

- Ask them to tell you what it's like out there in 'their world'. Learn from them and sympathise with the kinds of pressures they are feeling. If you believe they are resisting peer pressure,[9] tell them that makes you feel proud.

- Faced with the barrage of sexual messages hitting our teenagers, parents could be forgiven for feeling a lack of confidence, but don't be afraid to talk about what you believe. BUPA says, 'Talk about the emotions as well as the physical process, and *explain your own beliefs and values*.'[10] The former chief editor of one of the teenage magazines put it like this: 'You really want to say, "These are my values; these are our family's values. This is what I hope you will do." This is a very powerful message. Teens don't want to disappoint you.'[11] At the very least your input will give them a view that will challenge others they receive and that will help them make their decisions.

- Be careful about the way you talk about people who have different values to you. If you use derogatory language about celebrities, or even friends of your teenager who have chosen a sexual lifestyle you don't agree with, she will remember. Perhaps one day she'll make a decision she knows you wouldn't approve of. The last thing you want her to feel is, 'I couldn't tell my mother – she'd call me a slag.'

- Be sensitive to your teenager if they don't have a boyfriend or girlfriend. It's easy to feel left on the shelf at thirteen, and the pressure to bag somebody (anybody!) can be intense. Again, this pressure doesn't just come from their peers, but from the media messages that target teens: 'How to get the man of your dreams,' 'How to make yourself irresistible to girls.' Some teenagers end up in sexual relationships before they really want to because they think it's the only way they are going to attract somebody.

The role of parents is often to bring a balance to the other messages our teenagers are constantly getting and to encourage them to develop wide interests and lots of friends of both sexes. The truth is, though, that when all you want is to be snogging for Britain, having your father going on about the joys of a single life is not normally what you want to hear. It's usually a lot more effective if your teenagers have some role models – perhaps older teenagers or people in their early twenties – who have decided they don't want to get attached at the moment, but are obviously confident, fulfilled and enjoying life.

Sex

Finally, we should remember that most parents want to teach their teenagers not just about sex, but about love and commitment. But it may be that our children make sexual choices which we would not approve of, or want for them, and that our love and commitment *to them* is about to be tested. When we meet parents who have faced and come through such situations, they may not have dealt with things perfectly, but they do tend to have stressed, above all, that whatever their children have done, they are still loved.

Byron told me of the day his sixteen-year-old daughter told him she was pregnant. He said,

> *I actually felt my knees go weak and I was about to yell at her, but then I stopped myself. I took a deep breath and just put my arms around her. We both cried for ages. And after a while I said, 'I love you and I love you just as much now as I always have. And Mum and I will be with you – whatever.'*

Dear Jason,

I have been unable to sleep since I broke off your engagement to my daughter. Will you forgive and forget?

I was much too sensitive about your Mohawk, tattoo and pierced nose. I now realise that motorcycles aren't really that dangerous, and I really should not have reacted that way to the fact that you have never held a job. I am sure, too, that some other very nice people live under the bridge in the park.

Sure, my daughter is only eighteen and wants to marry you instead of going to Harvard on full scholarship. After all, you can't learn everything about life from books.

I sometimes forget how backward I can be. I was wrong. I was a fool. I have now come to my senses, and you have my full blessing to marry my daughter.

Sincerely,
Your future father-in-law

P.S. Congratulations on winning this week's lottery.

7

The Internet

As long as there have been teenagers, the task of parenting them has involved grappling with the tension of wanting to know as much as possible about what they are up to and realising that sometimes it's better not to know. But having said that, the past few years have seen the introduction of a new area of teenage life where many parents have almost zero knowledge of what's going on. Without doubt the Internet has revolutionised our lives – much of it for good. We shop, book holidays, chat and get information that we used to spend hours scouring libraries for. And yet we all know that there are negative aspects – and not least for children. Childnet International,[1] a charity dedicated to children's Internet safety, categorises the dangers of the web for children into three distinct areas: Content, Commercialism and Contact. Most of us, as parents, understand the dangers of inappropriate content (such as pornography), and with more and more young people accessing Internet content on their mobile phone, parents are quickly recognising the commercial pressures (and are often having to foot the bills!). However the third issue – contact, where children might come into contact with a stranger who threatens them or seeks to meet up with them to abuse them, is a growing fear which is being amplified by the new phenomenon of social networking.

Sites such as Bebo, MySpace and Teenspot are not just a mystery for parents, but for many teachers as well. They are somewhere where teenagers can swap ideas, gossip and photographs, and drool over *X Factor* winners away from the prying eyes of adults.

They are all different, but essentially they work like this: you register with your name, address, email and phone number and then fill in a personal profile which will cover things like your favourite music, bands, films and any other interesting bits which will appear on your 'homepage'. You can design your homepage in your own style, including photographs, and are encouraged to add your school. This can only be viewed by 'selected direct friends'. Bebo suggest that if you are under twenty-one you do not elect to make this page public – but if you do, the information is open to any other registered user. Once you are up and running, you will have access to hundreds of other school clubs and thousands of other users.

It's not hard to understand how such sites can become popular. Will Gardner, the research and policy manager for Childnet, put it like this: 'These sites can be fantastic environments for kids. They can express themselves, talk about their music tastes and what's bothering them, and communicate with each other.'[2] But then he went on to say, 'What we are concerned about are the potential dangers and risks involved and the lack of awareness some children might have.'

Those risks are real and have to do with the fact that whereas the challenge of the Internet used to involve preventing children from accessing unsuitable content, it is now that teenagers are producing their own content which may have inherent dangers. It was this that worried Linda Wybar, the head teacher of a girls' school in Kent. More than seven hundred of her pupils have signed up to Bebo, but she called in the police when she discovered that some of them were not only revealing personal details, but posting photographs of themselves on it that she considered 'indecent'.[3] One sixteen-year-old girl had submitted a photograph of herself in a swimsuit on her bed and had given enough personal information for a reporter from the *Daily Mail* to discover her address and phone number within minutes.[4] The fact is that many teenagers elect to have their homepage made public and therefore open to any other registered user.

Linda Wybar then wrote to every parent about her concerns: 'Most girls who have registered have included a potentially dangerous amount of personal detail, including full names, names of friends and, perhaps most worryingly, a photograph. Some of these photographs could only be described as soft pornography when viewed by the wrong people. We feel this lays the girls open to potential paedophiles.'

She's right. A spokesperson for the Child Exploitation and Online Protection Centre, a new Government funded police centre, said, 'There is a phenomenal growth in social networking sites, and young people have been putting personal information there which could easily identify them. We don't want them to put that kind of information online – because that's where young people go – so do paedophiles.'[5] One such teenager is Georgina, aged thirteen. She has a computer in her bedroom. Her homepage says that her best friend is Sophie and her favourite bands are the Scissor Sisters and Lily Allen. She likes watching *Little Britain*. She has begun showing pictures of herself in suggestive poses. She says that when somebody starts 'chatting' online and says, 'Wow U look hot!' it makes her feel good. She has already met face to face with some people she first encountered on the site and intends to meet more.

This is an edited extract of an Internet chat on a social networking website that raised concerns at the Child Exploitation and Online Protection Centre:[6]

ST*R boy   *I'm horny J how u feelin?*

Angelgurl   *(embarrassed) lets talk bout somfink else*

ST*R boy   *cm on angel . . . bet u is an angel. Turn on ur cam*

Angelgurl   *k. but u turn it on 1st. I am an angel really!*

TEENAGERS!

ST*R boy   *cm on, b fun . . . yeah. That's it, that's nice. U pretty*

Angelgurl   *fanks J*

ST*R boy   *I wanna c more . . . take that top off??*

Angelgurl   *u rude*

ST*R boy   *whats ur mobile? I'll send u a pic.*

Angelgurl   *I can't give u that; my mum wud kill me*

ST*R boy   *wot kind of m8 doesn't give digits?? I can't take u out if u don't give me ur numbers*

Angelgurl   *my mum would be mad*

ST*R boy   *ur mum's neva gonna knw. What happens between us stays between us right?*

Angelgurl   *yea*

ST*R boy   *cum on angel . . . show sum skin*

Angelgurl   *u r 2 intense – turn on ur cam so I can c who u r*

ST*R boy   *it's broken – but I'll send u a pic if u give me ur mobile? How will u recognise me otherwise wen I come 2 urs??*

Angelgurl   *u don't knw where I am*

ST*R boy   *yeah I do angel. I know exactly who u r & where u r. I'm gona drive up 2 u now*

The Internet

Angelgurl *How can u drive – u 16??*

ST*R boy *Got my provisional*

Angelgurl *u lyin?? U 2 old 4 me?*

ST*R boy *nah angel. I'm perfect 4 u*

Angelgurl *I'm going now. Ur weird*

ST*R boy *I'll find u again angel – I wana chat more*

Angelgurl signs off

According to police sources more than fifty thousand sexual predators are thought to be online at any one time.[7] And of the eight million children in the UK with access to the Internet, one in twelve says they have gone to meet someone whom they initially encountered online.[8]

This is how one teenage girl described such an encounter:

One of my friends went on a chatroom and started talking to a boy. He said he was fifteen and had blonde hair and blue eyes. They started sending emails every day. First I was fine about this because I thought they were mates, but then she started showing off that she had a boyfriend. I asked who,

107

and she said he was called Jake and was the person from the chatroom. I asked if he had sent a picture of himself. She showed me a picture and I realised that the boy was a model in the magazine I was reading. When I looked at it closely, I could see where 'Jake' had cut out the pic. The next day my friend came in. She was really scared because 'Jake' had asked her to meet him. At first I wasn't going to let her, but in the end I went with her. When we got to the meeting place, we saw a thirty-year-old man.[9]

In June 2006 a man became the first person to be convicted of child grooming offences after one of his victims alerted the police. He had arranged to meet a fourteen-year-old girl for sex. By the time police intervened he had already enticed and had sex with two other girls aged thirteen and fourteen. He had met his victims in the chatroom of the website Teenspot.com.[10]

You may say, 'Not my teenager!' But are you sure? And how would you know? It is estimated that over 60 per cent of thirteen- to seventeen-year-olds in the UK have personal pages on social networking sites. Of these, 46 per cent claim to have given out personal information, while only 5 per cent of their parents realised this. A third of them have received unwanted sexual or offensive comments – though again only 5 per cent of parents had any knowledge of this.[11]

Professor of Social Psychology Sonia Livingstone says to parents:

> *Eight per cent of young users who go online at least once a week say they have met face to face with someone they first met on the Internet and 40 per cent say they have pretended about some aspect of themselves online. Parents need to be more aware of the risks their children are facing.*[12]

What an incredible dilemma this is for parents. Even when we come to realise the dangers, it's not easy to know what to do about it: but do something we must. This is not marginal: it affects the lives of most teenagers – probably *your* teenager. John Carr, advisor to the children's charity NCH, put it like this:

> *The gap between what children are actually doing and what their parents think they are doing is a lot larger than many people would have imagined. It is*

a gap we must try to close. Parents are always going to be the first and best line of defence and the most effective means of support for children who get into difficulties. For them to do that properly and adequately, they need to have an understanding of the Internet.[13]

Thames Valley Police put it rather more chillingly:

As responsible parents or guardians you would never leave a child alone in a strange area, let them visit a city unsupervised, let them enter adult-only shops or clubs, or meet a total stranger. Unfortunately, every time the child in your care logs on to the web without supervision they face the same potential dangers as they do in all the situations above.[14]

I quite understand that if your child is fifteen and has been using the Internet almost as much as they have been eating, then the chances of their accepting a tutorial from a parent (even if we could give it!) are slight. Nevertheless, knowledge doesn't always mean they will act wisely, and even with older teens it's well worth finding out what they are doing on the web and trying to help them create a safe environment. With younger children especially, it's important to get involved at the very beginning.

Here are some steps that can help:

- Encourage your child to use a chatroom that requires registration the first time you visit. These are also more likely to have 'moderators' – people who keep an eye on what is going on and have the ability to exclude people who are breaking the rules.

- Explain that even after they have registered, they should never give out their email address or phone number to somebody they do not know. Encourage your child to use a nickname and also to be careful not to give out their friends' details. One expert put it like this: 'Would you put a billboard around your neck with your name, age, mobile phone number and address on it and walk down the street?'[15]

- Some sites allow children to build up a list of 'selected friends'. These are other users that your children trust and allow to chat with them. Talk with your children about what they might want to be sure of before they invite somebody to join their 'selected friends'.

- Warn your teenager to be aware of somebody who wants to get too close too soon – perhaps someone asking for personal details (such as an address or phone number) or someone who wants them to send a photograph or use the webcam, or who sends photographs of themselves which make your teenager feel uncomfortable.

- Sending photos is fine – to people your teenagers actually know. But remind them that they should never send their photograph to somebody who is just an 'Internet friend'. In many ways these people are still strangers and may have been deceptive about themselves. Also remind them that when they send a photo via their mobile phone, they are normally sending their mobile phone number as well.

- Tell them to always let you know if somebody has made them feel uneasy – perhaps by inappropriate language or suggestions. Incidents can be reported to your service provider or to the CEOP centre at www.ceop.gov.uk

- Remind your child that they should only meet face to face with somebody they have 'met' online if they have an adult they trust present – and then only in a public place.

- Warn them about chatting online with somebody who is obsessed with secrecy. They may insist you don't tell anyone about their chats with you or ask you to keep details of a proposed meeting secret.

- Remember that even though most teenagers would prefer to have a computer in their bedroom with Internet access, this may not be wise. Having a computer in the living room or somewhere else where people are coming and going makes it a little harder to get into trouble.

- Consider installing filtering software that prevents your teenager entering sites that you don't wish them to. Remember, though, that most teenagers will have access to the web at Internet cafes or friends' houses – which is why it's essential they understand *why* the safety rules are important.

It's true that teenagers who don't use the Internet at all face the fewest risks in these areas, but they are also missing out on the incredible opportunity of accessing the libraries, museums, universities, sports stadia, rock concerts and so much more that make up the world city that is the web. The UK *Children Go Online* report stated that restricting Internet access to our teenagers is a poor strategy for minimising risks. I think they are right, but the dangers are real, nevertheless. This is an area where as parents we have to do our homework, get up to speed – and get involved.

8

Drugs

We have already talked about parental fears, but for many parents the fear of drugs is greater than all the rest. There's hardly a mother or father in the country who has not gasped at the face of Leah Betts, whose parents took the courageous decision to allow a photograph of her in hospital, surrounded by tubes and equipment, to appear in newspapers in the hope that other young people might be deterred from using the same drug.

But sometimes the fears are just that – *fears*. I heard of a father who found a small white tablet in his son's room. He immediately thought the worst but, in fairness, instead of giving his son the third degree when the boy came home from school, he took the tablet to the local chemist. The pharmacist looked at it gravely and after a suitable pause said, 'Mr Clarkson, I think you've discovered a Smint mint!'

The truth is that the vast majority of teenagers are not, nor ever will be, addicted to drugs. Nevertheless, your child will not get through their teenage years without being offered drugs and they already know somebody who is taking them.[1] The harsh reality is that the UK has some of the highest rates of alcohol, tobacco and illegal drug use amongst fifteen and sixteen-year-olds in the whole of Europe.[2]

But if drugs are so bad, why do teenagers take them? Here are some reasons:

- To rebel or shock people
- To feel they belong to a group of friends
- They enjoy taking risks[3]
- It's fun
- It's the in-thing to do
- They are easy to get hold of
- It's part of a night out – maybe a rave
- It feels and looks grown-up
- It's an escape from the pressures of life
- They are bored

And as well as these reasons, we need to understand that there is a much more fundamental reason: teenagers – or anybody for that matter – take drugs because *they work*. In the short term they give you a buzz; they make you feel good. Drugs work for the person who is looking for a good time at a night club, they work for the girl who is constantly bullied and wants the pain to go away for a while, and they work for the person who needs relief from the constant and relentless pressure of their employment.

But how can we help our teenagers to say no to the short-term buzz of drugs for the sake of being saved from the negative effects? In a society where drug use is so easy, how can we give our children a fighting chance of staying drug free?

The stakes are high. One study showed that the rates of alcohol dependency were four times higher among those who started drinking at the age of fourteen than those who started aged twenty – so every year is precious.[4] However, a survey by the charity Action on Addiction found that one in four children say their parents are ill-informed in this area and their best source of information is the media. The survey also found that 40 per cent of parents leave the job of educating their children about drugs to schools and the police.[5]

A drugs strategy for parents

1. Know about drugs

Steven Lanzet, a clinical consultant working in the area of chemical dependency, said, 'There are clearly things that parents can do . . . the first step is to educate themselves.'[6] One of the most common things parents say to me is, 'I can't talk to my kid about drugs – they know more about them than me!' That may be true, but if it is we dare not let it stay that way. The biggest problem with the education part is not the actual getting of information – which these days is easier than ever – but for many parents it's over-coming the psychological barrier to believing that this is an area we want to enter. Perhaps we feel that even by talking about it, we acknowledge the awful possibility that our teenager could be taking drugs.

But if we are to help our teenagers, we need to learn what drugs do – both legal (like tobacco and alcohol) and illegal (like cannabis, cocaine and heroin) – how they make people feel and what the short- and long-term effects are. We shouldn't limit that knowledge to the drugs themselves. We need to find out what drugs education our teenagers are getting at school and perhaps even talk with the police to discover what the special dangers are in the area in which we live.

For many teenagers the totality of the drug education they have received from their parents is 'Drugs will kill you!' The problem with this is that for most teens, tomorrow seems light years away, never mind the distant prospect of having lung cancer or a brain addled through cannabis use.

For some parents this education process may seem overwhelming, but there is plenty of information available in libraries, health centres, schools and on the web. And a word of warning: don't get too hung up about trying to learn the slang, or 'street names' as they change constantly and if we get them wrong our credibility factor will drop considerably!

2. Be ready to spot the symptoms

Before we go any further with this section let's just remind ourselves of the dangers of a drugs use 'tick list'. When I was a child we didn't have many books in our home, but one we did own was called simply, *The Doctor's Book*. This was a large red tome that gave the symptoms and possible treatments for the more well-known (and a couple of totally obscure) ailments that could blight any family. The only problem was that everybody in my family who consulted it immediately became convinced that not only did they have the illness they had looked up, but possibly the one on the facing page as well!

We can have the same problem with reading lists of the symptoms of drug use. I remember hearing of a mother who watched a television documentary on young people and drugs. She immediately rang her son's youth worker:

'I think that Tom might be taking drugs.'

The youth worker was astonished. There were several kids in the youth club he was pretty sure were taking stuff, but Tom would have been the last on his list. 'Why do you think that?' he asked.

'Well, apparently one of the symptoms of drug use is having sudden mood swings – and Tom has been a lot like that lately.'

The youth leader laughed, 'Mrs Ainslee, Tom is a

teenager – mood swings are what they do!'

But this mother was not to be put off: 'It's not just that. The programme talked about teenagers who become isolated from the rest of the family, and Tom is always in his room. And then it went on about them not wanting to communicate, and I tell you, for the past couple of years neither his father nor I have been able to get two words out of him. I've searched his room, but I didn't find anything. Perhaps he keeps them someplace else.'

'You did what!'

But having given this warning, there *are* some changes in behaviour that might be a sign that something is wrong.[7]

- Lack of energy – feeling tired all the time
- Eating problems
- Unexplained or sudden change to a new group of friends
- Changes in physical appearance, e.g. reddened eyes
- Dropping out of previously enjoyed activities, e.g. sport
- Mood swings

- Valuable items or money missing from the home
- A drop in school performance or truancy
- Silence, sulking or anger towards others

Again, let's stress that with the exception of money going missing, all the above symptoms (especially the last one!) could be put down to just being a normal teenager who is experiencing some emotional pressure – perhaps over friends or schoolwork.

3. Talk about drugs before it's an issue

If we are wise, we'll spend a fair amount of communication in listening, but teenagers want to hear their parents' thoughts on the subject. Of course, the best way to talk to a teenager will vary from family to family and with the age of the child. The aim should be to inform and warn. Having said that, scare tactics, such as 'You'll go blind within a week' don't normally work, and we increase the possibility of our teenager being made to look stupid in the eyes of their peers.

One of our goals during these times is for our teenager to build up their own knowledge. It can be very empowering for teenagers to know more about drugs than their peers and may well allow them to be a little more secure in saying no. Our conversations could start by picking up on what our teenagers are learning at school or, as we saw in conversations about sex, a storyline in one of the TV soaps.

When we talk with our children we need to share our own views and why we hold them. Whatever our opinions, we need to let our children know what our personal boundaries are. The really scary thing in this area is not that children are not paying attention to us, but that they *are*. The simple truth is that their behaviour will be influenced by ours. This is definitely one area where 'Do as I say, not as I do' doesn't work. If we use drugs, our children are more likely to. This is not only true of illegal drugs, but legal ones as well. If we smoke, they are more likely to. They will watch how we use alcohol and if the first thing they see us do when we get home from a stressful day at work is to pour a glass of wine, they will remember this.

4. Make their friends welcome in your home

There may come a time when you come to believe that it is positively dangerous for your teenager to mix with certain friends, and you may be wise to do all you can do discourage them from seeing those friends. But generally, make your teenager's friends welcome even if they wouldn't be your ideal choice. If you ban them from seeing them, they will probably do so anyway. In any event, some parents have found that the fastest way to get their daughter to ditch a boyfriend they don't approve of is to say to her, 'We really like him!'

5. Build your teenager's sense of personal value

In the battle against drugs, the sense of personal worth your teenager has is vital. This is a subject that we will look at in detail later in the book, but one way to do this is to show them that you value their opinions – actually listening to them when they talk and giving them space to articulate what they believe. When we do this we increase their sense of security in what they think.[8] Our goal is to encourage them in the belief that they can make their own decisions and don't have to go along with the crowd.

From the youngest age possible let them know that you are interested in them. Know who their friends are, their teachers' names, and their ambitions and fears.[9] If a parent has shown consistent interest in a child, then concern about drugs in the teenage years is not so easily seen as 'prying into my life'. And unless it's absolutely necessary, don't go searching for drugs in their bedroom – if your teenager finds out, the sense of betrayal and resulting loss of trust can be devastating.

6. Look out for 'vulnerable moments'

We need to be aware of times in our teenagers' lives when they may be more vulnerable to unhealthy behaviour. It could be a time of bereavement, family breakdown, exams, bullying or breaking up with their first boyfriend or girlfriend. It can be easy for a young person to turn to drugs to alter how they feel about a situation rather than deal with it. If we are aware of what life is throwing at them, we can be prepared to offer support, and perhaps cut them a little more slack than normal in less important areas.[10]

7. Allow other adults that you trust to be a support to your child

It can be hurtful when our teenager wants to talk to another adult rather than ourselves, but so long as we can trust that person we should encourage it. Let's face it, there are things you'd rather not share with *your* parents, and we should be grateful for the fact that they are happy to talk to another person in whom we have confidence.

What happens if we discover our teenager is taking drugs?

I'm tempted to say, 'Don't panic' but the truth is, panic is an understandable reaction – though not a very effective one. We'd have to be a particularly cool customer not to allow ourselves to lurch headlong into a doomsday scenario – today cannabis, tomorrow speed . . . cocaine . . . heroin. On the other hand, we'd be foolish not to take it seriously. Here's what one father said:

> *The sheer feeling of helplessness and of despair is beyond measure. There will probably be an*

overwhelming feeling of failure and loss of control. These are all natural and understandable reactions and so the first and hardest bit of advice is: don't lose it. We will probably be thinking it's all our fault, but the truth is, we could be the best parent in the world and our teenager may still decide to try drugs. In order to give them the best possible support, we need to wait until our own emotions are under control first. Too many parents have lived to regret the words, 'That's it! Leave my house and never come back!' when they never really meant it in the first place.

We'll need to talk with our teenager, but it's vital to pick our moment. Don't even begin to try and talk about it if they are currently under the influence. It's impossible to hold a sensible conversation with anyone drunk or high. These are big issues and it may be we are going to have just one chance to get this conversation right. It's not a good idea to risk that precious opportunity being lost because we are either incandescent with rage or an emotional wreck with grief. We need to take some time to think about what we will say. Our priority at this time is making sure of our child's safety and health.

Choose a time when you know you won't have any interruptions – perhaps even when you're driving them somewhere they want to go. Don't accuse them, because if you are wrong, you may well damage your long-term relationship. Let them know your concerns – perhaps you've found something in the house or are worried about changes in their behaviour. Perhaps say something like, 'You don't seem to have been your normal self lately. Have you been feeling OK?' Give them an opportunity to respond, but you may find they don't want to talk about it at all or are obviously lying. Don't give in to the temptation to get angry.

Try not to be judgemental or to ridicule, saying things like, 'How could you be so stupid?' The aim of this conversation isn't to pour out blame or even to punish, but to find out what is really going on in our teenager's life and help them make any changes they need to. It's important they know that our main concern is their wellbeing, not worrying about what the neighbours might think. Having said that, a softly-softly approach may not always be possible. Some situations call for us to consider not just the welfare of our teenager but the health and safety of the rest of the family – maybe younger siblings especially. It may be that we have to set down some rules – particularly in regard to what goes on in the home – and consequences if they are broken.

Some of us are going to need support ourselves to help us get through this situation. If our child is travelling down the path towards drug dependency, an experienced counsellor can not only help with the practical matter of how to deal with it, but also bring a sense of perspective. They will have dealt with many families who have both faced and come through these situations.

Finally, realise that even if you do find a joint of cannabis in their bedroom, then although it is a real cause for concern, it doesn't mean they are addicts or that they will necessarily become addicts. As we have seen in other areas, for most teenagers these experiences – dangerous though they are – are *experiments*, not lifestyle choices. Perhaps above all, remember that wonderful line from the book, *We Need to Talk About Kevin*: 'Sometimes you have to love your child the most when they deserve it the least.'

9

Self-esteem

Close your eyes and imagine you are a teenager again. Remember how desperately you wanted to be accepted by your peers and to look as cool as possible. Now fast forward a generation and imagine you are Chloe, aged fifteen. Chloe is attractive, bright and yet constantly feels like the pits compared to her seemingly more attractive peers.

One day at a party at a friend's house, Chloe notices a crowd around a computer screen. She can hear roars of laughter, groans and comments like 'Minging!' or 'Lush!' She stands on tip-toe to see what all the fuss is about. Ten of her friends have logged on to the website of *Bliss*, a magazine for teenage girls. They are gazing at a page entitled, 'How Sexy Are You?' *Bliss* invites its readers to submit their photographs and then asks other teenagers across the world to rate them on a score from nought to ten.[1]

The girl on the screen at the moment is very attractive and has accumulated an average score of eight. Various friends of Chloe's are rushing home to get photographs they can scan into the computer and, pretty soon, Chloe too is rummaging through her mother's family album to find one of herself she can live with. The image of her face hits the website at 10pm on Saturday 19 August. Over the following week Chloe and her friends gather in the evening to check the *Bliss* ratings. Most of her friends do pretty well with scores of seven plus. Perhaps Chloe just chose the wrong photograph. Over the coming months her entry draws hundreds of votes. Her average score is two.

Over those months Chloe's parents have become increasingly concerned about her. Whereas she used to enjoy sport and loved spending time at the nearby stables, she now seems to have lost all interest in her hobbies. Her grades at school are falling and they are worried that she is being bullied. She seems to have taken up with a set of girls who are constantly getting into trouble. They fear that she is sleeping around.

Is it the case that doing so badly in the 'How Sexy Are You?' website started Chloe on a downward spiral? Possibly not, but it was, without doubt, a devastating experience for her and it was one more pressure she could have done without. Since she was six years old she has been bombarded by media images that tell her how she should look. As she moved towards her teenage years the magazines she read invited her to scrutinise photographs of celebrities who had been caught off guard – their spots, greasy hair and cellulite helpfully ringed in red. Chloe is one of the 42 per cent of teenage girls who have considered cosmetic surgery. In a recent survey over half of the two thousand girls questioned wanted a tummy tuck; just under a half wanted thinner thighs; but Chloe was in the 15 per cent who believe that a nose reconstruction would transform not just her looks, but her life.[2]

In another survey nearly 60 per cent of girls aged fourteen to fifteen were unhappy with their weight, as were more than half of twelve and thirteen-year-olds.[3] One girl put it like this:

As a teenage girl I'm all too aware of the constant pressure to be thin.[4] I have to admit that on many

133

occasions it has crossed my mind how easy it would be to stick my fingers down my throat after my dinner, but I am proud to admit I have never given in to the temptation . . . perhaps that's the problem with today's society – we're all looking for the quick and easy way out.[5]

However, it's not just the girls. In the same survey, between a quarter and a third of boys said they wanted to be slimmer. The number of recorded cases of eating disorders among boys is lower than for girls, but it's climbing. And for boys, the pursuit of the perfect physique isn't confined to losing weight. Dr Heather Gardiner, a psychiatrist at the Gartnavel Royal Hospital in Glasgow said,

Boys, unlike girls, have three body images to consider: fat, thin and muscular . . . Go to your nearest health food shop and you'll be confronted by shelves of Olympian Fat Metaboliser, Body Fortress, Super Male Plex and other supplements with equally macho-sounding names.[6]

Dr Pat Spungin of *Raising Kids* seems to agree: 'In a previous generation, someone like David Beckham would have been lauded for his talent on the field. Now what he is doing is extending his brand to encompass his appearance. I think young boys pick up on that. It's not enough to be an ace footballer – you have to be a good-looking ace footballer.'[7]

Of course, all this is not just about looks. For many, the teenage years are a time of uncertainty and this affects almost every area of their lives: 'Am I a good friend?' 'Am I good at school?' 'Will I ever be able to get a job?' This is important stuff. People with low self-esteem (or, if you like, negative feelings about themselves) may be badly treated by others and are quite likely to treat *themselves* badly. This could manifest itself in eating disorders, teenage pregnancy or even suicidal thoughts.[8]

At such a time, when the stakes are so high, who is our teenagers' best hope for giving them a healthy self-esteem? Who can give them the best chance of coming out at the end of the teenage years with a measure of balance? According to a recent review commissioned by the Joseph Rowntree Foundation of all the available research regarding self-esteem, the good news and the bad news is the same: it's us – their parents![9] Psychotherapist Andrea Scherzer agrees; she happens to be talking about eating disorders but what she says has a much wider application for the whole of our teenagers' sense of worth: 'It is with the guidance of parents and other adults in close contact with teenagers that they can learn to shift the focus of their negative preoccupation with body shape, to that of building inner strength and self-confidence.' She emphasises, 'These girls need to learn to *value* themselves first.'[10]

I think Andrea Scherzer's use of the word 'value' is significant. The opposite of this is 'worthlessness'. My mother wasn't academic by any means but, having said that, she was one of the wisest people I have ever met. She and Andrea Scherzer would have got along just fine. I remember when I was about thirteen she said,

> I know you have to mix with kids who have more than we do, but I want you to know that you are as good as them. You are not better than them – treat everyone with respect – but you are as good as them. God loves you just as you are – as you get older you may appreciate how special that is – and for what it's worth, so do I.

I once saw a most dramatic illustration of the opposite

influence: the awesome power of a parent to create a negative sense of value in a child. When I first met her, Emily, a single woman, was in her forties. She was not only reserved, but painfully so. When she did speak, it was often with a biting tongue. At other times she would respond with a simple grunt. She dressed so as to not only make herself look unattractive, but at least fifteen years older than her actual age. She walked with a slight stoop. But Emily was something of an enigma; that sullen, unattractive face held the most incredible eyes.

Emily never drank alcohol, which perhaps explained what occurred on a Tuesday night at a party in the house of a friend. Very simply, she thought the punch was non-alcoholic; it wasn't. After two glasses she sat next to me and then did something I had never known her do before: she began to talk like a normal person. There was none of the usual sarcasm about the other guests, the standard of the food or the colour of the jacket I was wearing. Emily looked, in some ways, as if she was too weary for all of that, and instead a wistful look came into her eyes and she began to tell me about her childhood.

Her father had died when she was nine years old,

but the memories she had of him were good ones. He would often come home from work, look her out as she played in the garden, and sweep her into his arms and tell her he loved her. If he was late coming in and she had already gone to sleep, he would slip into her bedroom and sit on the end of her bed. She remembers sometimes stirring and saying sleepily, 'Hello, Daddy. What are you doing here?' His reply was always the same, 'I'm watching you and thinking how beautiful you are.' And then he would tuck the blankets tight around her, straighten the top sheet and just sit there, silently. Emily never felt more secure in the whole of her life, knowing that even as she slipped back into sleep, he was there.

I had been put down by this woman so many times I was scared of saying the wrong thing: 'You must miss him.' I don't know what I expected her to say – I suppose anything except, 'When he died, a part of me did too.'

'Why do you say that?'

She rummaged in her handbag and produced a black and white photograph. I took it from her and gazed into the eyes of one of the most beautiful teen-age girls I have ever seen. She took it from me.

'I was lovely, yes?'

'More than that,' I said, '. . . utterly beautiful. But why do you say a part of you died when you lost your father?'

'Because my mother loved me with the wrong kind of love.'

'What do you mean?'

She sighed: 'When somebody loves you with the wrong kind of love you can never please them. When you do badly, it makes them cross and they can't wait to tell you where you went wrong. When you do well, it simply reminds them that you could be even better if you tried harder, and so you never hear their pleasure. And after a while, unless you are very strong, you become the person they think you are and the real person dies. My father saw all the good in me and couldn't stop talking about it. My mother always wanted me to be better than I was. My mother's love only wanted to change me. If I came in the top ten at school she would tell me that if I worked harder I could be in the top five. She told me my skin was poor because I didn't get enough fresh air, and my hair was thin because I didn't eat enough fish. Once, when I was sixteen, I saved for three months for a dress to wear to the end-of-term ball. When I came downstairs in it she told me it made me look cheap. I remember going to my room, sitting on the end of my bed and cutting it into little strips.'

'Is she still alive?' I asked.

'No, she died five years ago. Her last words to me were, "Your glasses are on crooked."'

Won't you ever come first?

The results of the way Emily's mother tried to motivate her were devastating, but we should all acknowledge that the challenge of discovering how to best help our teenager to achieve his or her potential is not an easy one. Of course we want them to be the best they can be and a sense of personal achievement is important.

When we achieve things – it could be passing examinations, learning to play the saxophone, playing netball or just learning how to take a decent photograph – it gives us what psychologists call 'self-efficacy'; this is a confidence in overcoming challenges and engaging with the world. When people do not have a strong sense of self-efficacy the slightest failure will cause them to give up and they will be afraid of taking on any new challenges. Such a mindset leads more easily to anxiety, depression and helplessness, whereas people with a high sense of self-efficacy will persevere with tasks, being prepared to take a few knocks along the way.

The problem occurs when we so badly want our children to achieve that we fall into the trap of making them believe that our love for them is based on how well they do – 'performance based' – or even on how attractive they are. This can have severe effects on our teenagers. One psychologist put it like this: 'If you bring your children up to believe that the ultimate goal in life is to achieve academically, then they will feel good or bad about themselves depending on how many examinations they pass.' If you are constantly saying, 'Who couldn't love you? You are so pretty!' it may be hard for them when their looks fade. He said, 'When our kids are small, we may say, "Look – you've tied your own shoelaces! You are so special!" That's probably not a big deal, but if we carry on down that road – giving the impression that their personal worth is tied up in how well they do things – they will come unstuck the moment they fail at anything.' A healthy self-esteem is about valuing yourself for *who you are*, not what you can do. It's what psychologists call 'intrinsic self-worth' – a belief that we have value irrespective of what we achieve or how others regard us.

Having said that, putting it into practice is sometimes not so easy – as I found out for myself one evening when I tried to instil the principle into my own teenager. The night before Lloyd's GCSE results (that's 'I hate books' Lloyd), I told him I wanted a bit of a chat with him. I could see a look of panic on his face as if to say, 'Oh no! Somebody has told him something about me.'

I hastened to reassure him, 'I'm not going to have a go at you over anything.' He looked relieved.

I went on, 'Big day tomorrow, Son.'

He nodded – as if he thought a nod was safe.

'I just want you to know that I hope you've done well, but if you get ten A-stars I won't love you any more, and if you fail them all, I won't love you any less.'

He mumbled something at me and later said to a friend, 'It made me feel good, although if I'd known that at the beginning, I wouldn't have done *any* work!'

Having had a laugh at my clumsy efforts, it is vital,

nonetheless, that we build a sense of personal worth in our teenagers that is not related to performance. In my work I constantly come across people – often men, in their mid-life years – who have little inner peace because they are constantly trying to prove themselves. One man said to me, 'I remember running home from school and yelling, "Dad! I came second in the music exam in the whole of our county." My father said, "Won't you ever come first?"'

Of course, at the other extreme it may be dangerous to tell your teenager that he is fantastic at everything – if you set the bar too low, there is no real achievement – and also dangerous to build up his ego irrespective of his attitude to responsibility or the needs of others. One psychologist put it like this: 'If we're not careful as parents, we manage to raise cocky kids who think they are the bees-knees, but have no real foundation on which to sustain the knocks that life gives. It's quite a shock to some teenagers in their first job to find that employers who are looking for a team player aren't quite as crazy about their "I'm the centre of the universe attitude" as their parents were.'

So how ultimately will our teenagers perceive whether or not they have value? Some time ago I listened to a discussion on the topic 'What is the Greatest Question in the World?' As you can imagine, there were as many suggestions as there were people in the room and they ranged from the tongue-in-cheek, 'Why do you never see a baby pigeon?' to the philosophical, 'What is a question?' Near the end of the debate an older man spoke. He had been the only one so far not to give an opinion, a fact which may have added to the authority in his voice: 'The greatest question for any man or woman is this: "Am I loved?"' He said that a positive answer to this question had sustained people in the most horrendous situations in life and a negative reply meant that no amount of money or prestige could bring happiness.[11]

I don't know whether he was right, but I believe that the phrase he suggested is the biggest question for almost every teenager. At a time in our lives when so much is changing, and when we feel insecure in many areas, we want at least to know there is somebody who loves us – unconditionally. The way in which teenagers answer that question is the subject of our next chapter.

There are ten words that every parent of teenagers ought to say as soon as they wake in the morning and whisper under their breath before they close their eyes at night. These words are relevant whether your child wakes you most mornings with a cup of tea and says, 'How are you doing, today? Anything I can do to help?' or if your child is driving you and everybody else crazy at the moment.

Write these ten words on your office blotter; write them in felt pen on your fridge; write them on your heart . . .

*. . . Don't take all the credit;
don't take all the blame.*

10

Unconditional love and acceptance

How do teenagers answer the greatest question in the world? The truth is that they perceive it by our attitudes and our deeds; the things we say and do, and the way we behave towards them in the everyday. The world outside may judge them harshly in a dozen different categories, but pretty soon they will begin to perceive whether or not their parents, at least, look at them differently, in short, whether in their home, they are loved unconditionally.[1]

It could be in regard to looks. When parents reinforce the idea that a teenager's worth is closely tied to how attractive they are, they have no haven from the 'tickbox' judgements they find elsewhere. I once heard a father say of his slightly overweight daughter, 'Here comes, Jumbo.' He laughed as he said it and so did his daughter – although hers was a nervous laugh.

And our children will not only notice how we speak to them, but how we value others. If a father singles out one of his daughter's friends and describes her as 'the pretty one' or 'the chubby one', or if he describes a colleague as 'the one with the tatty clothes', he may, without realising it, be teaching a value that says people are worth more if they are physically attractive. And if he does this, he shouldn't be surprised to see his daughter waiting with bated breath to see how she's done in the *Bliss* 'How Sexy Are You?' survey. After all, she has come to believe that these are not just the values of some glossy magazine, but those of her own father.

Giving teenagers a sense of their value

Children who perceive they are valued have come to believe that although their parents want them to do well at school, their parents' love and approval is not based on the grades they get. They have never heard their father say, 'Unless you work harder, you'll never be as good as your sister.' Those who feel valued may well have a dozen rows a week with their parents over the mess they leave in the kitchen or the fact that they smoke, but they will also frequently hear their parents praise them for things they do well; they will be used to being caught doing something *right*.

It doesn't need weighty things to build a sense of being valued. Teenagers who are valued, occasionally hear their parents ask for their opinion. Something in a teenager's heart tells them that slowly the roles are changing. And they are right. The day will come faster than we dare think when they will have to look out for us, and when we seek their advice we confirm this changing status: 'Kim, I'm just not sure how to handle this. What do you think?' When we do this, we give them value. We may say, 'What would you do if you were me?' At first they might be embarrassed by such a request and brush it off with, 'How do I know? You're the adult!' But as we go on asking about different situations, and especially if they see us sometimes acting on their advice, they grow in confidence.

Sometimes it won't be just asking their opinion, but putting ourselves into their debt. We are so used to doing things *for* them we forget what it does to somebody's sense of value to believe that they are needed. To be effective this normally has to be asking them to do something a little outside the normal routine – not the dishes, for example – but perhaps a hand fixing something or trying to get a letter just right – something that gives the sense of another 'adult' helping out.

We give them a sense of personal value if we help them see that 'Those who die with the most toys wins' is a silly slogan. (In any case – wins what?) A long time ago, a wise carpenter put it like this, 'Your life doesn't just consist in the accumulation of the things you possess.' If material possessions are vital to us for our own sense of self-worth and our children watch us desperately trying to keep up, not only with the Joneses but with everybody else on our block, then they will grow up believing that the house they live in, the car they drive and the clothes they wear are all vital for their sense of wellbeing. This will be OK until they are made redundant. And that's the really scary thing about parenting teenagers: we are not just trying to mould their characters when they are sixteen, but also trying to help lay foundations that will stand them in good stead when they are in their thirties and beyond.

Our children will watch the way we handle our

disappointments. Our natural tendency may be to shield them from the harder events of life, but seeing their mother or father believe that life is worth living after the job loss or the divorce is a lesson in value they may never forget. That may mean sharing with them where we feel we have got it wrong. Use the 'Batman' analogy. Tell them that when you are young you believe that Batman wears a mask because he is a mysterious hero, but when you become an adult you realise it's so that if he ever totally screws something up, nobody will know who he is! When our teenagers see that we can make mistakes, say things we shouldn't, and simply foul up but still keep going, we teach them a vital life lesson. It's quite a thing to discover that your mother or father doesn't have all the answers – but that life still goes on.

I am not good at DIY and I never have been. When I was fourteen, the teacher in my woodwork class at school told us that for that term's final examination we could either make a coffee table or a potato plunger. I don't blame you for not knowing what a potato plunger is – neither did I, nor did I care, until I saw how complicated the coffee table looked. A potato plunger is used to, well . . . plunge. It makes a big hole in the ground into which you insert . . . a potato.

I gave that potato plunger everything I had and finally I laid it on the bench waiting for the teacher to walk around and inspect our work. When he reached me, he looked at my offering, sniffed, and said, 'What is it?' I remember thinking how unfair that was – it obviously wasn't the coffee table.

'Sir,' I said, 'it's a potato plunger.'

He replied, 'It's awful.'

I said, 'I did my best.'

Then he said, 'Parsons – your best is not good enough.'

I have often thought about his reply. Where do you go in life as a fourteen-year-old boy when your *best* isn't good enough?

When it comes to feeling valued, children are all too aware how the system works. In school, the honours are given to those at the top of the academic pecking order; in sport they know that the kids who break the tape first, get the silver cups; and with regard to their friends, it's the best looking who get the boyfriends and girlfriends first. But teenagers with a sense of their own value are able to say without doubt,

Unconditional love and acceptance

'My parents accept me, anyway.' That 'anyway' doesn't mean their mother and father don't encourage them to do better at school, or that they wouldn't prefer them to be more willing to help with the washing-up. It certainly doesn't mean that their parents approve of their every action. But it does mean the teenager knows that at the bottom of it all, at least with their mother and father, they are accepted for who they are – and are therefore loved.

These principles are not only vital for the child who makes a poor potato plunger or comes last in the races. They are equally important for the teenager who comes top in everything and wins every race they enter. And this is because they, too, need to learn that although their success is wonderful, their worth as a person does not lie in that success. And when the dreadful day comes, as it surely will whether they are sixteen or thirty-six, and they come in second – they will know that they are still *somebody*.

None of this is easy, for at least two reasons. First, it's hard to devote ourselves to creating a sense of value in our teenagers at a time of their lives when they may be treating us badly – not good for *our* sense of value![2] Second, just at the time when we try to show them that we value them, it may seem that *our* opinion matters least of all – that it's the opinion of friends, teachers, or even the parents of other children that they really care about. But this is an illusion: when we create a deep sense of value in our teenager we are giving them a *foundation* from which they will assess other people's opinions of their lives.

Dispelling the great illusion

People judge whether or not they are loved by whether or not we give them time. Life is busy for most of us. The demands of running a job, a home, and keeping body and soul together, can be all-consuming. Sometimes we say, 'I'm doing it all for them. I want them to have more than I had.' The sad truth is that our teenagers will forget the fancy computer we bought them, but will remember little things – things that didn't cost much, but where we had fun together. One father put it well: 'We are so busy giving our kids what we didn't have, that we don't have time to give them what we *did* have.'

When they are young, kids are suckers for the 'We'll do it later' routine:

'Dad, can we go fishing today?'

'Not today, Son. We'll do it next weekend. I'm busy just now.'

Helping our teenagers feel valued means that we give them not just time, but *attention*. One father told me that when he's talking to his teenage son for any length of time he switches off his mobile phone (incidentally, the son doesn't!). He said, 'I want him to know that what he is saying to me matters – that he deserves my attention.'

During any one year I speak to thousands of men and women in seminars based on my book, *The Heart of Success – making it in business without losing in life*.[3] Sometimes we are together for a whole day, but whether it's a day or just an hour, there is a point during the talk where I know without doubt that I have the attention of every single person in the room. It's where I say something like this:

> *Above all, remember that a slower day is not coming. We say to ourselves, 'Life won't always be this busy. One day I'm going to have more time – when I've passed my examinations, when the extension is completed, when I get promotion,*

when the new office is up and running.' But we should know that this 'slower day' is an illusion – most of us are driven by busyness from within. If you have anything at all that matters to you, make time for it today. It could be a phone call to a brother, sister or friend you haven't spoken to for a long time and most days you've intended to do it: do it today. If you want to learn to speak Spanish, send off for the brochure today. And if spending time with your partner and kids is important to you, make time for it now.

After the September 11th tragedy in New York City, people began to tell others what their loved ones, who had been trapped in the twin towers in New York, had said to them in frantic telephone conversations or email messages. Those who received calls from mobile phones from the doomed planes also told their stories. Some re-listened to messages left on answerphones. And as they shared their experiences, it was immediately evident that the same three words kept coming up time and time again. Those words did not refer to size of salary or bonuses, nor to the type of car recently purchased or expensive holidays taken. No. Lovers said them to lovers, husbands to wives, friends to friends and parents to kids: 'I love you.'

'Tell Suzanne, I love her.'

'Don't you forget that I love you.'

When it comes down to it, relationships are more important to most of us than anything else on the face of the earth; it's just that with the busyness of life we sometimes don't live as though that is true. Relationships take time. And relationships with teenagers take inordinate amounts of it. I agree that sometimes it's not quite as pleasurable as when they were small, because at least *then* they wanted to be with us, but it is time and it does cost. And it's necessary for reasons beyond the actual activity – be it standing on the touch-line of a football match, helping with homework or just shopping together. Stephen Covey talks about an emotional bank and the fact that when we share experiences with another person we put deposits there.[4] It is almost certain that you and your teenager will go through some periods of conflict and when that happens it will be important that there are memories of good times that you've spent together – in other words, that there's something in the bank.

Spending time is not easy with all teenagers. Some

will just leap with joy at the thought of an evening out with the old man; others would rather die a slow, painful death. But even with the latter kind, time together is important – though it takes a little work and sometimes a little guile. My two children couldn't have been more different in this area. I have made many mistakes as a father, but one thing I did get right was that most weeks, from the time she was twelve to about sixteen, my daughter Katie and I would go for a coffee together in the foyer of a local hotel. In some ways it was almost like a date. It was an adult setting, not expensive, but special enough to make her feel good, and we would just talk. When Lloyd hit twelve I tried to do the same with him but I couldn't get a word out of him. He'd drink his coffee in under a minute and just sit there scowling. That was until we swapped to a hotel with a pool table. We still didn't talk much apart from 'Pass the chalk,' but at least we were together. In his later teenage years Lloyd would sometimes wake me up at midnight and say, 'Do you fancy going for a curry?' I suppose he was using my device in reverse – he wasn't dying for conversation, but he did want an Indian. Most nights I climbed out of bed.

It's best to grab even a little communication when it's going. We'll look at it in a little more detail in the next chapter.

When You Thought I Wasn't Looking

When you thought I wasn't looking,
I saw you hang my first picture on the refrigerator,
and I wanted to paint another one.

When you thought I wasn't looking,
I saw you feed a stray cat, and I thought
it was good to be kind to animals.

When you thought I wasn't looking,
I saw you make my favourite cake for me,
and I knew that little things are special things.

When you thought I wasn't looking,
I heard you say a prayer,
and I believed there was a God
that I could always talk to.

When you thought I wasn't looking,
I felt you kiss me goodnight,
and I felt loved.

Unconditional love and acceptance

When you thought I wasn't looking,
I saw tears come from your eyes
and I learned that sometimes things hurt,
but it's all right to cry.

When you thought I wasn't looking,
I saw that you cared and I wanted to be
everything that I could be.

When you thought I wasn't looking,
I looked . . . and now I want to say thanks
for all the things I saw,
when you thought I wasn't looking.

11

Communication

British Telecom once ran a brilliant advertising campaign with the slogan, 'It's good to talk!' Most parents would agree, but sometimes it's not easy. Wendy's first child was Clare, who just loved to chat about everything; her second – Sam – wasn't quite as volube!:

> *My son seems to have turned doing nothing into a fine art. Ask him what he's done today and it's 'nuthin'. Ask him what he's doing later and he doesn't know. When pressed it'll probably be 'nuthin much'. His inactivity deserves praise for its stress-relieving properties, its silent contemplation interrupted only by the flick of a remote control, the clunk of the fridge door or the rhythmic beat of*

the soundtrack on his games console.

His concentration on 'nuthin much' is absolute. Food is the only thing which distracts him momentarily, either when moving his mouth to acknowledge his need of it, or moving it at a slightly increased speed to eat. Even his chewing never really gets beyond first gear.

He does go out with friends who have also been doing 'nuthin much'. They come to the house to agree on where they'll go to do 'nuthin much' and then go off together to do it. I suppose they have 'nuthin much' in common.

The power of words

It may be hard, but communication is vital and the truth is that at some level we're all doing it. Even the teenager with his 'nuthin much' was communicating! But our words can build relationships or destroy them. Most of us discovered in adulthood what we always suspected in childhood: that the little rhyme we had recited in the playground – 'Sticks and stones may break my bones but names will never hurt me' – could not have been more inaccurate. Many of us would be willing to swap the hurt caused by words for that inflicted by a fist. Our deepest and greatest hurts are usually caused by what others say to us and particularly so if they are said by people who claim to love us.

This is all especially relevant in the teenage arena, where conflict between children and parents is frequently a way of life: words are often flying fast and furious. Added to which, this is a time when our children are at the most cocky, know-it-all stage of their lives and just asking for a bit of sarcasm or a timely put down. But we should be careful. The teenage exterior often looks harder than the centre – and the ego is easily bruised. Our teenagers will survive, 'You haven't washed for days!' but comments that attack not their behaviour but their *person* – 'You are going to end up as a total loser!' – may do more lasting damage. And it's not always a good idea to precede giving criticism with praise about something else as this tends to diminish both, but overall our children need to hear positive things from us as well as negative.

The rules are different here from other areas of life. Our conversations with our teenagers – even the difficult ones – have a secret element that is not present in those we have with others. We are part of their learning process – the guinea pigs, if you like. With us, more than with any of their other relationships, they are using words to see what works and what doesn't. We want them to respect us, but we also want them to learn to defend their own corner. We want them to agree with us, but we also want to be part of helping them form their own opinions; we want them to give way to us, and yet realise that on us they are practising the skill of standing their ground. Do we want to win all our arguments with our teenagers? Well, at our lowest moments, definitely yes – but in truth we see their need to savour a few victories. As in other areas, they are not only learning the arts of life from us, but practising them *on* us. One girl said, 'I know sometimes that I really have a go at my parents, but if I did it with anybody else they'd hit me, sack me or never speak to me again.'

Don't be too hard on yourself. It's all very well my writing these things in the quiet of my study, rather like the football pundits who criticise the referee from the haven of the studio and with the benefit of watching the replay, but the parent, like the referee, has to react in the heat of the moment. And parents, like referees, need to forgive themselves for the odd bad decision. The truth is, it's not just our teenagers who are learning on the job; we as parents are trying to work out just how to communicate with this person who is on such a steep learning curve. I think of one single-parent dad who used to yell at his son every time he came home late. He said it was like water off a duck's back. But then one night this man blurted out to his son how it made him *feel* when he was late and didn't ring. He said, 'I feel helpless and afraid. If you just gave a quick ring to say you were on the way it would really help.' He said it worked. A mother told me how powerful it was that in the middle of a row with her teenage daughter she suddenly said 'Sorry.' She said,

> *I didn't just say it for effect. The truth was, both my daughter and I had worked ourselves up into this almighty rage and it was just stupid. We'd said things we didn't mean that were really hurtful and I thought, "I'm the parent here. If this was a conversation with a friend, one of us would have apologised by now." I thought I should at least show*

her that you can do that while still keeping your dignity. It not only changed that row, but a few weeks later my daughter apologised to me. I suppose I had shown her that adults can say sorry.

Of course, one of the most frustrating things about trying to communicate with some teenagers is that the only time they want to do it is at one o'clock in the morning! But sometimes we can't be too fussy about timing – often they don't have the skill of linking the importance of the subject to the convenience of the hour. I think of a mother whose fifteen-year-old son came to her in the kitchen one day after school; she was in the middle of getting dinner ready. He suddenly blurted out, 'Mum, I think I may be gay.' She said,

I was rushing round doing a million things and then I thought, 'He may have been agonising over telling me this for months, but I have only ten seconds to respond. He may remember what I say for the rest of his life.' We sat down and talked for an hour.

Those talks with our teenagers don't always have to be long, but they are often significant, especially if we are prepared to open ourselves up to them – our fears, our mistakes, and occasionally even stories of when we were their age. Some teenagers are amazed that their parents had similar experiences to the ones they are now going through – like the mother who told her fifteen-year-old daughter that when she was the same age a boyfriend finished with her because she said she wouldn't sleep with him.

In this area as well, we find to our horror, as we have discovered elsewhere, that values are *caught* even more effectively than they are *taught*. Our children are watching how we communicate with others – with our husband or wife, with colleagues or friends. We can show them how to use words to encourage and lift others, to build bridges with them. But it is also true that if we use words like weapons they will learn that art too.

The power of touch

Communication is more than words: touch plays a part. Some years ago a teenager wrote to me and said, 'My parents don't hug me any more because they think I'm too old. But when no-one is looking, I wish they still would.' This isn't easy for parents, because even as we do try to give them that hug, our teenager may be standing with his arms pinned to his sides and grimacing as he used to when having to kiss powdery aunties when he was small. It *is* important we do it when nobody is watching – especially their friends – but it is vital that we do it; that through touch we convey our affection. It could be as simple as a touch on the arm, but we ought not to swallow hook, line and sinker the impression that they never want us to go near them again.

A couple of years ago I was invited to speak to some of the inmates at a prison. These men had read a book I wrote some time ago, *The Sixty Minute Father*, and in weekly parenting classes had been discussing some of the issues it raised.[1] As I stood before them that day I can tell you quite honestly that I felt totally inadequate for the task. The looks on the prisoners' faces and their body language seemed to say to me that they agreed with my own assessment of my competency. What did I know about being a father while in prison? How could I enter into what these men were feeling and the special pressures on their families? And yet I desperately wanted to help them. I knew that they were suffering for the wrong they had done and yet, in addition to their personal regret – which was often very evident – their families too were paying a very high price. The opening lines of the talk I'd prepared seemed far too trite. And then as I looked at them a thought struck me and I began like this:

> *I know you do not choose to be in this institution – it is in fact the last place you want to be – but you* have *chosen to be with me for this session on parenting. And therefore you have done today what many fathers don't do in the whole of a lifetime – you've taken some time to ask yourselves the simple question: 'How can I be a better father?'*

I sensed the atmosphere change almost immediately. During the session I told them about a businessman I had met who told me that he wasn't the emotional kind and couldn't bring himself to hug his children. I said that I'd suggested to him that he practise in front of a mirror! At the end of our time together one of the men approached me and said, 'The visiting room in the prison is cold and uninviting. When my family come to see me we sit around a table. That table and the four chairs that surround it are screwed to the floor. One of the chairs is red and the prisoner has to sit on it. The room has a children's play area, but it is in the corner and sometimes my child will call to me to join her playing there or perhaps she'll fall and need me. I get up to go to her and as I do a warder will shout, "Hey, you! Get back on the red chair." '

The prisoner then said, 'Tell the man who can't bring himself to hug his kids about the man who can't get off the red chair.'

The power of praise

Before we leave the area of communication let's take a moment to consider the silver bullet of speech. When parents discover this they can change forever the way their teenager looks at themselves and what they can achieve: it is the power of praise.

To believe that we matter is crucial for our mental and perhaps our physical health. And the main – perhaps for some, the *only* – way that children perceive this is from their parents. When they are young we are normally very aware of this need. For this reason we heap praise on paintings of cows with five legs, eat with relish awful-tasting cakes baked by six-year-old hands, and treat wins in school races as though world records have been broken. But so often when our children become teenagers we stop doing this. There may be many reasons for it. One is that they can be so rude to us that half the time we just don't feel like it, but also we have a sneaking suspicion that they are beyond all this praise stuff. We are wrong: we may feel more detached from them, but they desperately still need to be told they are loved and valued, and one way they perceive this is by our giving them praise. In the teenage years especially they need to grow in independence, but they also need to know that their parents continue to empathise with their needs as they did when they were younger. Intellectually they want to be treated like adults, but emotionally they are still children. Affirmation from us makes it less likely for them to crave it elsewhere – perhaps from their peers – at any cost.

Some time ago I set up a consultancy that has had the opportunity to influence thousands of companies, many of them blue-chip. A couple of years ago we were seeking to appoint a senior consultant and had an application from an outstanding candidate. He was an Oxford graduate, had advised both governments and companies across Europe, and spoke several languages fluently. I felt as if he should have been interviewing me.

During our time together it emerged that we had gone to the same primary school. I asked, 'How was school for you?'

His head went down. 'Traumatic,' he said.

I wondered what could have gone on – I remembered the school as a pretty normal place. 'What happened?' I asked him. This was his reply:

> *On the second day of school the teacher gave us all a bean bag and told us to stand in a circle. We had to throw our bean bags in the air and catch them. On the last occasion I threw my bean bag up but it didn't come down. Perhaps another child grabbed it while it was in the air or it got caught in a gutter, but at the end of the lesson the teacher made me stand in front of the class and told everybody that I had lost my bean bag.*

This man in his mid-forties had done it all. He was, by any standards, a high-achiever, and yet the memory of what happened to a five-year-old boy was still very strong. Before you laugh at him, remember that you too have your stories – those people, who, when you were seven or seventeen, crushed you with their words. And unless you are very unusual, you were changed in some way by what they said. Of course, we need criticism – how else will we learn? But we need it from the right kind of critic and there are always two kinds.

The first criticise to bring us down. They do not have our good at heart and sometimes it seems as if they enjoy the criticism too much. A work colleague says, 'I'm just telling you this for your benefit' but we sense 'our benefit' is the last thing on their mind. The second kind of critic tells us where we are going wrong with the sole aim of building us up. They genuinely want us to do better – they are truly on our side. Of course, the great dilemma is how do we tell which is which? It's not that difficult. Those who criticise to build us up will always praise as well as blame. They look for opportunities to tell us when we have done well. Sometimes we even sense the praise is a little over the top – they are so keen to encourage us.

We discovered in the business world years ago that if you want to build a great company you have to have managers who are sufficiently emotionally secure in themselves to praise as well as blame. Jill Garret, who used to be the Managing Director of the Gallup Organisation, says: 'People don't leave jobs, they leave supervisors,' and so often that is because with these managers there is always criticism and never praise. Few of us can survive in a climate like that.

Unfortunately, many teenagers feel like that about their parents. They say to friends, 'They are always on my back over something or other. If it's not my music, it's my clothes or what I do on the weekends. I can never please them.' It's hard not to have some sympathy for parents in this situation – after all, with many teenagers there doesn't seem much around that deserves praise; life is pretty grim. But praise is still necessary – if only to convince our teenagers that we belong to the class of critic who is on their side. It helps them to say, 'They do keep on to me, but I know at heart they are for me.'

When opportunities for praise are thin on the ground, we have to look hard to find them – but find them we must. Sometimes it's not a bad idea to re-mind your teenagers when they did well: 'I remember when you made us that meal – it was brilliant.'

Communication

'Hey, remember when you made us laugh till we were sick?'

Praise lifts all our heads. Sometimes it's good for our teenagers to overhear us praising them to somebody else.

Great teachers have learnt the power of praise – and the need to find something that can be praised. I've already said that I wasn't very good at school and was reluctant to take part in class activity, but when I was nine Mr Thomas asked me to hold the paper as he used the guillotine in the art class. You had to keep it very steady. I did – and gave him a great edge. The next week he asked me to hold it again, and again the following week. Over the coming months I became his sole helper on the guillotine. One day, just as we finished, he surveyed a stack of neatly cut paper and then turned to the other children and said, 'Robert Parsons is the best holder of guillotine paper in the whole of the class.'

Since those days I have done some interesting things: I have been one of the senior partners in a legal practice, written ten books and lectured all across the world. But almost fifty years later 'Robert Parsons is the best holder of guillotine paper in the whole of the class' is still firm in my mind. Why is that? Perhaps it's because when somebody encourages you, no matter how seemingly insignificant, your mind is opened to the wonderful possibility that there could be other things out there you could do. Mr Thomas was a brilliant teacher. He knew that although blame is necessary, you also have to search for opportunities, however small, to praise. He understood the sheer power of affirmation.

I understand the real world. And in that world we are normally, by necessity, on our teenagers' backs over some issue or another. But none of us can survive if all we hear is criticism. Once in a while it's important to try another tack: *catch them doing something right* – and praise them for it.

When they were small you clapped when they sang. Don't ever stop.

Liam's Lift

'You want a lift home then, do you, love?'

'Umm, yeah. I suppose so.'

'Well, you can't walk all that way and there's no bus.'

'Yeah, but, well . . . don't be early.'

'No, I'll be on time.'

'Yeah, but don't be early and sit in the car and wave.'

'No, okay. I'll pretend I don't know you.'

'Cool. But don't be tempted to get out and come and watch the end of the game. You've seen football before – you know how it's played.'

'But I'm interested, love. Don't you want me to be interested?'

'No. Not remotely . . . and don't wear your green coat.'

'Why not?'

'Well it's green . . . and whatever you do, don't go and chat to Mr Haffenden on the edge of the field and laugh at his jokes.'

'Why not? Mr Haffenden's very funny – I could do with a laugh!'

'No, he isn't, Mum. It's just him and the mothers in the PTA that think so. It's embarrassing.'

'Oh. Right.'

'In fact it might be best if you park round the corner outside Addison's and I'll come and find you, okay?'

'Oh. Okay.'

12

Letting them go

If it is true that one of the greatest battles for the parents of teenagers is the battle against fear, the heart of this fear is often that our teenagers will make a single mistake that will ruin their lives forever. The problem with fear is that it often takes us over, and never more so than when that fear is combined with a lessening sense of control over the lives of our children. We may be afraid that somebody will harm our six-year-old, but we can largely prevent that happening by keeping them near us and being watchful. We may have exactly the same fear for our sixteen-year-old, but here we have little control. We imagine them getting into an argument after a late-night party or accepting a lift from a friend who has been drinking.

That's just for starters. There's the fear they will fail their exams, get in trouble with the police or get in with the wrong crowd. And because we are afraid for them there is so much we want to warn them of. The only problem is that just at the time when we have so much we want to tell them, they seem often to have pulled up the communication drawbridge.[1]

Sometimes we may feel we just have to take matters into our own hands, which is exactly what Mrs Dora Hatt did. In 1936 the *Daily Mirror* reported the case of this mother whose fear about her son and sex was so great she asked the justice system to intervene.[2] She told the judge that her son had started 'courting a girl his own age' and was spending most of his wages on her. She said he was not getting 'proper sleep and proper food' and that he was undermining his health. In throwing out her case the judge said, 'Mrs Hatt, you can't stop a boy from seeing his girlfriend and if you try, you'll only make him want to do it all the more.' We may smile at her, but we should all recognise the terrible dilemma of wanting our children to become independent and yet being terrified that if they can't find their underpants, how on earth are they going to find their way to the job interview?

Letting them go

Letting go is hard, but it is absolutely vital. I remember witnessing a most amazing example of a mother achieving it. A television crew was filming the efforts of a golden eagle who was teaching her young to fly. The camera first zoomed in on the nest and we saw three balls of fluff that hardly looked in enough shape to take a waddle, never mind a leap into emptiness. But mother was determined. With two siblings looking on, the first eaglet was nudged to the edge of the nest. The sight of the fledging trying to resist a fully grown golden eagle would have been amusing were it not so heart-rending. You wanted to yell, 'That kid is not ready to leave!' But mother pressed on with her nudging and then suddenly flipped the eaglet right out of the nest. If this kid had had any flying lessons, he'd forgotten everything he learned and he fell like a stone. It's not that his wings weren't flapping – they were flapping for America – it's just that nothing was happening! And then we saw an amazing thing. When it seemed that junior's young life was drawing to an end, the mother swooped underneath his plummeting body, caught him on her wing and carried him back to the nest.

Over the following days, those who had the

patience watched that mother teach her offspring that they weren't meant to live in the nest – they were born to fly. And one day the spectators were rewarded. As they shielded their eyes and gazed up into an azure blue sky, they could see four eagles riding the thermals.

The controlling parent

If we close our eyes and imagine that incredible sight most of us would have a longing that we, too, would be able to launch our teenagers safely out of the nest. (Incidentally, one woman wrote to me and said, 'I hear all this stuff about empty nest syndrome – can you help me achieve it?') But there may be a deep problem. Some of us as parents have a characteristic that is almost certain to make the process of letting go agony for us and almost unbearable for our teenager: it is the need to control.

The problem is that control so easily masquerades as love. A mother may say, 'I am only doing this for your benefit.' A father will say, 'I don't want you to go through what I experienced.' But actually these are manipulations to get our way. These parents try to arrange, supervise and monitor every aspect of their child's life – from clothes worn, school work and friends thought suitable, to the kind of music acceptable and use of free time. The controlling parent loves their child, but it is love on a leash. So long as the child doesn't stray too far from what is acceptable to the parent, the relationship can have a semblance of success. But it is only a *semblance*, because few of us choose relationships with those who want to control us. Everybody wants to run from such people. Think of people in your own life who wanted to control you and ask yourself whether you enjoyed their friendship. They commented on the way you dressed, cooked, drove, spoke, and decorated your home. Eventually they suffocated you.

Psychologist Dr Madeline Levine talks of the tragedy that she sees daily in her counselling rooms as she talks with children whose parents love them, but will not give them the space to develop in their own way and at their own pace. These parents have crossed the line between support of their child and intrusion into their lives. She says that, just as when our children were toddlers it was important they fumble with their shoe laces while learning to tie them, so in teenage years it is vital for the adolescent to fumble with difficult tasks and choices. This is preparation for life when the parent is not around.

> Parents who persistently fall on the side of intervening for their child, as opposed to supporting their child's attempts to problem solve, interfere with the most important task of childhood and adolescence: the development of a sense of self.[3]

Levine continues,

> Support is about the needs of the child. Intrusion is about the needs of the parent. Mother birds know the value of nudging their fledglings out of the nest so that they learn how to soar on their own wings. Over-involved parents are clipping their children's wings.

In such a relationship the teenager has only two real options: capitulation for now or rebellion. I say capitulation for *now* because almost certainly the rebellion will follow, even if it doesn't manifest itself until the child is well into adulthood. I have often seen men who had strongly controlling fathers have their first real rebellion in their thirties. The problem then is that the form of rebellion is not having their nose pierced, but perhaps leaving a wife and children so they can 'find themselves'.

The controlling parent is often incredibly generous with money – in fact, to a fault. But there is little generosity elsewhere – particularly in the area of *trust*. John's first daughter got pregnant when she was fifteen and was now in her early twenties, but John was eaten up with fear that this was also going to happen to Kirsty, his second child. One night, when Kirsty, too, was fifteen, she got home a few minutes late. She was surprised to see her father on the corner of her street, looking angry. 'Where have you been?' he demanded.

'I've been around Julie's.'

'No, you haven't! You've been with that boy I saw you with last week – and I know what you've been doing!'

'Dad! What is wrong with you? I've been at Julie's!'

'Well, we'll soon see!'

Kirsty was frog-marched inside her house and watched open-mouthed as her father dialled Julie's number. She tried to protest, but he wouldn't be stopped. Her friend's mother answered. Kirsty stood by as her father tried to control his anger. 'Mrs Thompson? This is Kirsty's father. I'm sorry to bother you, but could you tell me who your daughter has been with this evening?'

Kirsty watched as her father listened, apologised, and slowly put the phone down. And then she burst into tears. 'You see! Just as I said! You just don't trust me!'

In my work I come across family situations in which the teenagers abuse their parents. These children lie, steal and sometimes physically attack their mother and father. Sometimes these extreme situations call for a suspension of general principles. Parents would be naive to trust such teenagers; experience has shown them time and time again that their suspicions are valid. But turning to more normal situations we can sometimes turn a child who is basically trustworthy into a teenager who believes their only hope of survival is to deceive us. We often do this by a desire for excessive control.

I think now of an extreme example. Jo was seventeen and asked her parents if the following Saturday she could go to a nightclub with some friends from school. After days of discussion, and to her surprise, her father agreed. The big night came and Jo was dancing on a crowded floor when suddenly her friend said, 'Isn't that your father up there looking over the balcony?' In a club full of teenagers and young adults, the solitary figure of a middle-aged man in a collar and tie stood out like a neon light in a monastery. Jo wanted to die that very second. When they got home he told her he was 'just checking'. That father is asking to be deceived.

None of this is easy. Some parents *may* need, in extreme circumstances, to search their children's rooms, listen in to their conversations or perhaps even read their diaries. But these things should never happen, not even once, in a normal relationship. The problem is that when the controlling parent does these things they almost always find something, hear something or read something that may in itself be quite innocent, but which actually feeds their need for more answers and more control. And anyway, which of us could survive surveillance at that kind of level without the discovery of a few things that are not quite so innocent? We are all – and that includes

191

teenagers – entitled to a few secrets.

The truth is that there are parental limits on both our responsibility and our power. Dr John White, psychiatrist and author of *Parents in Pain* put it like this, 'You cannot control another human being, even if that human being is your own child. You do not have the right to. You may discipline and teach; you may train; you may point out the right course; you may "shape behavior patterns"; you may reason; you may plead. But you cannot and may not ever control.'[4]

The End of an Era

. . . Then suddenly the end of adolescence arrives. You start to recognise 'nice' things about your children again. They have conversations with you. They even start *conversations with you. Those conversations become littered with phrases like, 'Can I help?', 'What would you like?' and 'I'll let you know.'*

It's hard at first. Like learning a new language. But you get the hang of it. The volume of conversations is lower, their length is longer and the words come out more slowly – sometimes even in a considered way. It's a revelation in communication. Not that they notice – but you do.

Increasingly they even ask for advice, even genuinely value your opinion. Sometimes they take one and weigh up the other. But they are not afraid to disagree with you either – they just do it without yelling. You respect each other. Occasionally they actually seem to like being with you and care about how you are.

TEENAGERS!

Then one day you wake up and realise that you've still got a son or daughter – but you have also got a very special friend you've known all their lives and half of yours. You breathe a sigh of relief. Like night feeds and tantrums, you've got through it, you're still alive . . . and you're still a parent.

As we close

For a moment, imagine that it's your daughter's thirteenth birthday party and for the last time you have candles on the cake. Friends and relatives, including a great-grandmother, smile as Rachel bends to try to blow them all out. Her breath hits the tiny flames and they begin to dance as they fight against dying. And it is then that you have the strangest experience. As you watch the flames they suddenly blur and you begin to consider what your daughter's teenage years hold for you. And in a moment you are catapulted forward two and half thousand days. It is your daughter's *twentieth* birthday and now you have the luxury of looking back. There are times of incredible laughter and joy, but then you gasp as the pictures change and you see yourself coming through difficult situations that if you asked yourself now, you would never believe you could have faced.

In my work I see tremendous pain in families. I know as well as any that there are no easy answers, but time and time again I meet parents whose children, when they were teenagers, practically broke their hearts. But they got those teenagers through and now they have a brief respite as they look back on the rapids from quieter waters. I say 'brief' because the really bad news is that for some reason the worries of parenting seem not to diminish as they get older. As I write, today's newspaper reports that the oldest woman in Britain has just died aged one-hundred-and-twelve. By her bedside as she died was her daughter aged ninety. I would love to know who was worrying most about whom.

All kinds of parents will have read this book. Some have children who are only eight or nine years old. You are wise to consider some of the challenges of the teenage years now – most of us spend our lives as parents playing 'catch-up'. Many others will have children who are just about to embark on the teenage years and some will be in the very middle of what seems to be a great battle – one that they appear to be losing. Try not to lose heart and, above all, remember one of our main themes: *this is not just you*.

Remember, too, one of our other themes – the one I mentioned at the very beginning: *just get them through*. No prizes for 'Best Father in Chichester' or medallions for 'Mother of the Decade'. Just a car clapped out with taxiing, a wallet frayed at the edges, and eyes so used to being propped open with matches waiting for our offspring to come in at night, they won't close anymore.

But perhaps the last few words should go to three teenagers. First, Kerry, aged fourteen:

> Parents need to understand that we want to stay out late, and we want somebody to care that we come in on time. We don't want anybody nagging us over homework, and yet we want somebody to push us a bit to get it done. We're too old to be hugged, but sometimes we want to be. We can do it all ourselves, but sometimes we feel like kids in junior school again. We want to be free and still know you're on guard. Parenting must be a hard job.

And finally, two quotes from the Chief Examiner's Report on Key Skills Communication Level 3 Test.[1]

The examination had asked the teenagers to identify significant problems that they face and to identify ways to reduce the pressure that many young people feel. As the Chief Examiner brought his report to a close he felt compelled to mention the contributions of two teenagers who had shown 'wisdom beyond their years'.

The first said, 'Parents know a lot more than teenagers – talking things through with them is a help. It's like counselling, but cheaper.'

And the second? Well, the candidate who ended his paper with the following exhortation to parents could, perhaps, be summing up the whole of this book . . .

Relax

Remove pressure

Have patience

Ask questions

Show you are there for them

Love

Love

Love

Now that really is worth an A-star!

Notes

Before We Start

1. As Levitt and Dubner put it: 'Fear is in fact a major component of the act of parenting.' See Steven D. Levitt and Stephen J. Dubner, *Freakonomics* (Penguin, 2005).

2. Peter Stearns, *Anxious Parents: A History of Modern Childrearing in America* (New York University Press, 2003).

Chapter 1

1. B. Bates et al., *Smoking, drinking and drug use among young teenagers in 2002: A survey carried out on behalf of the Department of Health by the*

National Centre for Social Research and the National Foundations for Educational Research (The Stationery Office, London, 2005).

2. *Young People and Alcohol*, Factsheet 8 (Alcohol Concern, 2000).

3. *Confiscation of Alcohol*, House of Commons Hansard Debates for 15 Jan 2003 (pt 12).

4. In *The Herald*'s January 2004 series on teenagers, celebrity teen Peaches Geldof acknowledges that, 'Society has become more materialistic and there is a lot of competition between teens of who has the coolest stuff. Consumerism drives the economy, and the market targets teenagers.' However, she goes on to make the point, 'But why blame us? Our parents are the ones who created it.'

5. Kay Redfield Jamison, *Night Falls Fast – Understanding Suicide* (Macmillan, 2000).

6. Six of the studies cited in J. Aldgate, *The Children Act Now, Messages from Research* (The Stationery Office, 2001), draw attention to the importance of social support and social networks in providing a cushion against adversity. In two of the family support studies Aldgate reviews, lack of emotional

support was the factor that tipped some mothers into depression.

7. In his book, *Paranoid Parenting*, sociologist Frank Furedi describes this in terms of a breakdown in adult solidarity. See F. Furedi, *Paranoid Parenting: Abandon your anxieties and be a good parent* (Penguin, 2001), p. 22.

8. In the 1950s, Peter Townsend calculated that three out of five older people in Bethnal Green belonged to 'three-generational extended families' – either by living with children and grandchildren, or by seeing them every day. Three decades later, the British Social Attitudes survey of 1998 found a mere 2 per cent of grandparents living in such households. Quoted in B. Brown and G. Dench, 'Extended Families: the heart of the private realm', in A. Buonfino and G. Mulgan (eds), *Porcupines in Winter: The pleasures and pains of living together in modern Britain* (Young Foundation, 2006).

9. This is especially the case in couples who are obliged to engage in what is termed shift- or serial-parenting, where they work at different times in order to manage childcare between

them. See I. La Valle, S. Arthur, C. Millward, J Scott and M. Clayden, *Happy Families? Atypical Work and its Influence on Family Life* (The Policy Press/JRF, 2002).

10. Hannah Green and Sophia Parker, *The Other Glass Ceiling: the domestic politics of parenting* (Demos, 2005), p. 96.

11. 'Isolation and loneliness: features of modern parenting', *Parentline Plus*, 8 March 2005: http://www.parentlineplus.org.uk/index.php?id= 28&backPID=14&tt_news=36

12. 'The Missing Link in Parenting Education and Support', Penny Mansfield, *One Plus One, The Bulletin*, Vol. 8(2), May 2004.

13. Anne Garvey, 'When the Children Leave Home . . .', *Guardian*, 5 March 2003.

14. http:/www.en.wikiquote.org/wiki/Margaret _Mead [not accessible]

15. Studies like that carried out by the Joseph Rowntree Foundation have highlighted problems common to lone parents generally, such as poverty, social isolation and lack of respite from childcare, plus additional problems of geographical isolation. See C. Hooper, *Rural lone parents:*

the evaluation of a self-help support project (Joseph Rowntree Foundation, 1996).

Chapter 2

1. The second wave of brain development, i.e. over-production of grey matter just prior to puberty, is described in J. N. Giedd, J. Blumenthal, N. O. Jeffries, et al., 'Brain development during childhood and adolescence: a longitudinal MRI study', *Nature Neuroscience*, 2(10), 1999, pp. 861–3.

2. http://www.brainconnection.com/topics/?main=news-in-rev/teen-frontal (accessed 20 August 2006) cites Dr Yurgelun-Todd who says, 'Good judgment is learned but you can't learn it if you don't have the necessary hardware.' This theme is covered in A. A. Baird, S. A. Gruber, D. A. Fein et al., 'Functional magnetic resonance imaging of facial affect recognition in children and adolescents', *Journal of the American Academy of Child and Adolescent Psychiatry*, 38(2), 1999, pp. 195–9.

3. http://www.youngminds.org.uk/magazine/64/neustatter.php (*Young Minds* Magazine, No 64, accessed 20 August 2006) describes the work of

Dr Elizabeth Cauffman, a psychologist at the University of Pittsburgh, who has been studying 1200 teens who have committed a serious offence. She has been trying to pinpoint the moment when the average teenager can make a reasoned decision. She has concluded that it is age seventeen.

4. Due to the relative lack of maturity in young people's frontal lobes in comparison to those of adults, Sowell et al. describe how it is not so much the frontal lobes as the more 'gut reaction' amygdala that is chosen by the teenage brain to process emotions. The latter area of the brain does not produce such reasoned perceptions and therefore performance in this area of processing is impaired. E. R. Sowell, P. M. Thompson, C. J. Holmes, et al., '*In vivo* evidence for post-adolescent brain maturation in frontal and striatal regions', *Nature Neuroscience*, 2(10), 1999, pp. 859–61.

5. Barbara Strauch, *Why are they so Weird? What's Really Going on in a Teenager's Brain* (Bloomsbury, 2003).

6. ibid.

7. Angela Huebner, Assistant Professor of Family and Child Development at Virginia Tech, explains that the cognitive changes that teenagers go through makes them tend to become very cause-oriented. Their activism is related to the ability to think about abstract concepts. They also tend to exhibit a 'justice' orientation. They are quick to point out inconsistencies between adults' words and their actions, have difficulty seeing shades of grey and see little room for error. *Adolescent Growth and Development*, Virginia Tech Publication Number 350-850, posted March 2000 at: http://www.ext.vt.edu/pubs/family/350-850/350-850.html (accessed 19 September 2006).

8. J. Brannen, K. Dodd, A. Oakley and P. Storey, *Young People, Health and Family Life* (Open University Press, 1994).

9. Nicola Morgan, *Blame the Brain* (Walker Books Ltd, 2005).

Chapter 3

1. Parents are, however, right to be concerned about certain types of experimentation, especially if it

occurs very early in adolescence. According to McVie and Bradshaw, early experimentation with alcohol, smoking and illegal drug use resulted in behavioural continuity for all three substances, demonstrated by the high proportion of drinkers, smokers and drug users at age twelve who continued to report such behaviours when they were followed up at later ages. See S. McVie and P. Bradshaw, *Adolescent Smoking, Drinking and Drug Use, The Edinburgh Study of Youth Transitions and Crime Report No 7*, 2005.

2. See also Chapter 2, note 7.

3. Bear in mind Furstenberg's point that in the earlier part of the twentieth century work experience constituted a majority, if not the majority, activity during adolescent years. Whether in farms, trade or factories, most youth were employed by their mid-teens. In other words, the historical expectations placed on teenagers would have left them with far less leisure time than is currently the case. See F. Furstenberg, 'Sociology of Adolescence and Youth in the 1990s: A Critical Commentary', *Journal of Marriage and Family*, 62(4), 2002, pp. 896–910. Popular novelist John

Grisham's book about growing up in 1950s rural America, *A Painted House* (Doubleday, 2001), extends this theme.

4. Academics like McVie and Bradshaw concur. Their longitudinal study of Edinburgh youth transitions and crime found that unsupervised leisure activities, such as hanging around on the streets, provide opportunities for getting involved in problematic behaviour. See S. McVie and P. Bradshaw, *Adolescent Smoking, Drinking and Drug Use, The Edinburgh Study of Youth Transitions and Crime Report No 7*, 2005.

5. See D. R. Weinberger, B. Elvevåg and J. N. Giedd, *The Adolescent Brain: A Work in Progress* (The National Campaign to Prevent Teen Pregnancy, 2005).

6. Research from the US found a direct linear relationship between substance use and various aspects of leisure and lifestyle, including peer substance-using behaviour, how much parents 'really knew' about their activities, and number of hours spent hanging out with friends (Caldwell and Darling, 1996) in *Adolescent Smoking, Drinking and Drug Use, The Edinburgh Study of Youth Transitions and Crime Report No 7*, S. McVie & P. Bradshaw, 2005.

7. In his review of the sociology of adolescence and youth in the 1990s, Furstenberg notes that most studies, in general, show that so-called adolescent problematic behaviours occur episodically (i.e. intermittently) and experimentally, rather than as ingrained patterns. See F. Furstenberg, 'Sociology of Adolescence and Youth in the 1990s: A Critical Commentary', *Journal of Marriage and Family*, 62(4), 2000, pp. 896–910.

8. John White, *Parents in Pain* (InterVarsity Press, 1979).

Chapter 4

1. C. Ritchie et al., *Aspirations and Expectations* (NFPI, 2005) make the point that although the Standardised Assessment Test (SAT) processes at the ages of 7, 11 and 14 are possibly instrumental in raising educational standards for most children (Buchanan et al., 2004), they may have the unintended consequence of labelling children from an early age into academic achievers and non-achievers.

2. P. West and H. Sweeting, 'Fifteen, female and

stressed', *Journal of Child Psychology and Psychiatry*, 44, 2003.

3. Oliver James, 'The Trouble with Girls', *Observer*, 1 June 2003.

4. ibid.

5. ibid.

6. Anthony Seldon, 'Stop the treadmill, I want to get off', *The Times*, 6 September 2006.

7. *San Francisco Chronicle*, 25 June 2006, a review of Madeline Levine, *The Price of Privilege: How Parental Pressure and Material Advantage Are Creating a Generation of Disconnected and Unhappy Kids* (HarperCollins, 2006).

8. Dr Terri Apter (*The Myth of Maturity: What teenagers need from parents to become adults*, Norton, 2001) explains how many academically able students are actually late learners in key areas of emotional intelligence. They may, for example, be so accustomed to success that they learn far later than their peers the important skill of how to maintain their spirit in the face of disappointment. They have also not learned how to tolerate being less than the best.

9. The importance of parental involvement in

children's schooling, especially where peer pressure discourages educational attainment, was highlighted by recent research on educational under-achievement. See *The Times*, 15 November 2006.

10. D. Clifton and P. Nelson, *Soar with Your Strengths* (Dell Publishing Company, 1996).

Chapter 5

1. A. Katz, A. Buchanan and V. Bream, *Bullying in Britain: Testimonies from Teenagers* (Young Voice, 2001).

2. 'Bullying – biggest ever rise in calls to ChildLine', 25 August 2004: http://www.childline.org.uk/ Bullying-biggesteverriseincalls.asp

3. A study, reported in A. Katz, A. Buchanan and V. Bream, *Bullying in Britain: Testimonies from Teenagers* (Young Voice, 2001), collected views from 7,000 young people, of whom more than half said they had been bullied, one in ten severely so, with a quarter saying that bullying was the main cause of stress in their lives.

4. OFSTED points out that although a distinction is

commonly made between physical and verbal bullying, they can occur together and verbal abuse can carry a strong threat of violence. See *Bullying: effective action in secondary schools* (HMI 465, 2003).

5. Research with eleven- to nineteen-year-olds found that one in five young people (20 per cent) had experienced bullying or threats via email, Internet chatroom or text message. Bullying using text messaging was the most common of these three forms of bullying, experienced by 14 per cent of young people. Almost three quarters (73 per cent) of young people who had been bullied by email, Internet chatroom or text message said they knew the person who bullied or threatened them, while a quarter (26 per cent) said it was done by a stranger. See *Putting U in the Picture* (NCH and TescoMobile, 2005).

6. Microsoft survey, quoted in the *Guardian*, 15 March 2006.

7. CBBC *Newsround*, 15 April 2002: http://news.bbc.co.uk/cbbcnews/hi/club/your _reports/newsid_1931000/1931438.stm

8. http://www.childline.org.uk

Chapter 6

1. 'Talking To Teens About Sex' (CBS News, 26 September 2005): http://www.cbsnews.com/stories/2005/09/26/earlyshow/living/parenting/main885473.shtml

2. In research conducted by the National Consumer Council children reported that they felt companies used inappropriate ways to sell to them, that sexual images used in advertising cause embarrassment and are used excessively. See Ed Mayo, *Shopping Generation* (National Consumer Council, 2005).

3. D. Paton, 'The Economics of Family Planning and Underage Conceptions', *Journal of Health Economics*, March 2002.

4. The SEU report states that the likelihood of teenage pregnancy is more than doubled for young women who did not discuss sex easily with their parents. See Social Exclusion Unit, *Teenage Pregnancy* (Cm 4342, HMSO, 1999). Beverley Hughes said that parents had to take the initiative by putting aside any embarrassment and starting a dialogue about sex with their children. See Lucy

Ward, 'Appeal to Parents on Teenage Births', *Guardian*, 26 May 2005.

5. This is very common. During the Social Exclusion Unit's consultation on teenage pregnancy, parents repeatedly said that they felt embarrassed and ill-equipped to broach this subject with their children. See Social Exclusion Unit, *Teenage Pregnancy* (Cm 4342, HMSO, 1999).

6. Wellings et al. state that earlier first intercourse is less likely to be an autonomous and a consensual event, and more likely to be regretted and unprotected against pregnancy and infection. See K. Wellings, K. Nanchahal, W. Macdowall, S. McManus, R. Erens et al., 'Sexual behaviour in Britain: early heterosexual experience', *Lancet* 358, 2001, pp. 1843–50.

7. A tracking survey to inform the National Evaluation of the Teenage Pregnancy Strategy surveyed more than 750 young people aged 13–21 across England in June 2003. It showed that only around four in ten had fairly accurate perceptions of the proportion of young people who had sexual intercourse before the age of sixteen. Forty-six per cent mistakenly believed

that more than half of young people had sex before they were sixteen. See *Evaluation of the Teenage Pregnancy Strategy. Tracking survey: Report of results of nine waves of research, October 2003* (BMRB International, 2003). The proportion of men reporting intercourse before age sixteen is around 30 per cent while the proportion of women reporting intercourse before age sixteen is around 26 per cent.

8. Steve Chalke, *The Parentalk Guide to Your Child and Sex* (Hodder & Stoughton, 2000).

9. To give some indication of how much of a challenge peer pressure actually is, the *Glasgow Herald* reports that when asked recently what was on their wish-list of subjects to be taught at school, almost half of the sixteen-year-olds questioned said that they wanted to be taught how to withstand the demands placed on them to conform. See *Glasgow Herald*'s special report on Teenagers, January 2004.

10. BUPA Health Information Fact Sheet, *Teens and Sex*: http://hcd2.bupa.co.uk/fact_sheets/html/ teen_sex.html?print

11. CBS News, *Talking To Teens About Sex* (New York,

26 September 2005): http://www.cbsnews.
com/stories/2005/09/26/earlyshow/living/parenti
ng/main885473.shtml

Chapter 7

1. http://www.childnet-int.org
2. Emma Cowing, 'The virtual teenage world where parents fear to tread', *The Scotsman*, 11 July 2006.
3. Paul Lewis, 'Teenage networking websites face anti-paedophile investigation', *Guardian*, 3 July 2006.
4. Neil Sears, 'Paedophile warning over teen web-sites bebo and MySpace', *Daily Mail*, 3 July 2006.
5. ibid.
6. Paul Lewis, 'Teenage networking websites face anti-paedophile investigation', *Guardian*, 3 July 2006.
7. ibid.
8. ibid.
9. CBBC Newsround, 'Be careful on the web!' (updated 15 July 2003): http://news.bbc.co.uk/cbbcnews/hi/club/your_reports/newsid_3068000/3068481.stm

10. Paul Lewis, 'Teenage networking websites face anti-paedophile investigation', *Guardian*, 3 July 2006.

11. The London School of Economics and Political Science, 'Parents still underestimate internet risks', 21 July 2004.

12. ibid.

13. Sally Kinnes, 'Secret lives of high-tech teenagers', *The Sunday Times*, 24 October 2004.

14. Thames Valley Police, *Chat Safe – A safety guide for internet chat rooms*: http://www.thamesvalley.police.uk/chatsafe/index.htm

15. Jim Gamble, Chief Executive of the Child Exploitation and Online Protection Centre quoted in Emma Cowing, 'The virtual teenage world where parents fear to tread', *The Scotsman*, 11 July 2006.

Chapter 8

1. The current estimate is that 26 per cent of pupils between the age of 11 and 15 have ever taken drugs and 19 per cent of them in the last year.

Of these 4 per cent took Class A drugs. Six per cent of pupils of this age group report having taken drugs once a month or more. See *Smoking, drinking and drug use among young people in England in 2005*: Table 9.11 (London, Home Office, 2004).

2. B. Hibell, B. Andersson, T. Bjarnason, S. Ahlström, O. Balakireva, A. Kokkevi and M. Morgan, *Alcohol and Other Drug Use Among Students in 35 European Countries, The ESPAD Report 2003* (2004).

3. Again, this is linked to the fact that the adolescent brain is not a finished product but a work in progress. The greatest changes to the parts of the brain responsible for functions such as self-control, judgement, emotions and organisation occur between puberty and adulthood: http://www. actforyouth.net (accessed 29 August 2006).

4. B. F. Grant and D. A. Dawson, 'Age at onset of alcohol use and its association with DSM-IV alcohol abuse and dependence: results from the national longitudinal alcohol epidemiologic survey', *Journal of Substance Abuse*, 9, 1997, pp. 103–10.

5. Action on Addiction, *'British parents' biggest worry*

is that their teenagers will experiment with drugs – survey findings', 28 July 2005:

http://www.aona.co.uk/news/news-statements/surveyfindings

6. ibid.

7. Provided by the Children, Youth and Women's Health Service, South Australia: http://www.cyh.com/HealthTopics/HealthTopicDetails.aspx?p=114&np=141&id=1747

8. Some researchers suggest that a relationship between an adolescent and an adult person becomes significant when the adult communicates the idea that the adolescent matters as a person. See J. Cotterell, *Social Networks and Social Influences in Adolescence* (Routledge, 1996).

9. Resnick et al. refer to such things as indications of parents' 'connectedness' to their children. See M. D. Resnick, L. J. Harris and R. W. Blum, 'The impact of caring and connectedness on adolescent health and well-being', *Journal of Paediatrics and Child Health* (29) Suppl 1, 1993 pp. S3–9.

10. In a pithy one-liner, Professor Jones sums up much research on youth transitions by saying, 'The availability of parental support depends

greatly on the quality of family relationships'. In other words, if parents get on with their teens they are far more likely to be supportive than if there is a high level of conflict. See G. Jones, *Young Adults and the Extension of Economic Independence* (NFPI, 2005). This makes sense – they are pushing you away, you feel as if your best efforts are thrown back in your face, but actually they probably need their parents' support most when the relationship is not as harmonious as you might like.

Chapter 9

1. *Bliss* magazine: http://www.blissmag.co.uk/how sexyami.asp
2. BBC News: http://news.bbc.co.uk/1/hi/health/4147961.stm
3. Tony Halpin, 'Class of 04 Fearful and Consumed by Worries', *Times Online*, 22 April 2005.
4. Girls aged between thirteen and nineteen account for 50 per cent of all anorexia and bulimia cases (*Young Minds Magazine* 69). Last year a survey of 300,000 school children by the Schools Health

Education Unit found that almost half of all teenage girls were skipping meals regularly in an attempt to lose weight.

5. 'Teens and Body Image', *Families*: http://www.familiesonline.co.uk/article/static/259

6. ibid.

7. http://www.raisingkids.co.uk/todaysnews/news_240505_01.asp

8. ibid.

9. Nicolas Emler, *Self-esteem: the costs and cause of low self-worth* (Joseph Rowntree Foundation, 2001).

10. BBC News, 'Teenage Girls Hate Their Bodies', 6 January 2004: http://news.bbc.co.uk/1/hi/health/3368833.stm

11. Foster and Sherr report that children in close and affectionate families that promote positive values are less likely to suffer the ill effects of poverty and deprivation than those growing up in families characterised by instability, conflict and neglect. Many growing up in vulnerable situations prove resilient in the face of adversity and that resilience is often a consequence of care provided by care-givers and families. When this intimate circle of care is functioning well it can compensate for

negative influences that arise from the wider environment. See G. Foster and L. Sherr, 'Vulnerability and resilience of children and youth', *Vulnerable Children and Youth Studies* 1(1), 2006, p. 1.

Chapter 10

1. Shulman and Scharf emphasise that parents remain a major source of support for their adolescent children even as the importance of peers' opinions increases. See S. Shulman and M. Scharf, 'Adolescent Romantic Behaviours: Age- and Gender-Related Differences, and Links With Family and Peer Relationships', *Journal of Research on Adolescence* 10(1), 2000, pp. 99–118.
2. Indeed, Langford et al. describe how teenagers' withdrawal from closeness can herald a parental identity crisis. See W. Langford, C. Lewis, Y. Solomon and J. Warin, *Family Understandings: Closeness, authority and independence in families with teenagers* (Joseph Rowntree Foundation, 2001).
3. Rob Parsons, *The Heart of Success – making it in*

business without losing in life (Hodder & Stoughton, 2002).

4. Stephen Covey, *The 7 Habits of Highly Effective People* (Simon & Schuster, 1994).

Chapter 11

1. Rob Parsons, *The Sixty Minute Father* (Hodder & Stoughton, 1995).

Chapter 12

1. Langford et al. found that teenagers were aware that parents invited communication from teenagers in order to maintain control as well as to provide support and friendship. It is worth bearing in mind that teenagers' own sense of being in control may lie in withholding inform-ation. See W. Langford, C. Lewis, Y. Solomon and J. Warin, *Family Understandings: Closeness, authority and independence in families with teenagers* (Joseph Rowntree Foundation, 2001).
2. *Daily Mirror*, 5 December 1936.
3. *San Francisco Chronicle*, 25 June 2006, a review of

Notes

Madeline Levine, *The Price of Privilege: How Parental Pressure and Material Advantage Are Creating a Generation of Disconnected and Unhappy Kids* (HarperCollins, 2006).
4. John White, *Parents in Pain* (InterVarsity Press, 1979).

As we close

1. Key Skills Communication Level 3 Test (Teenage Concerns), City & Guilds, Chief Examiner's Report, June 2006.

Hear Rob Parsons live on the secrets of parenting teenagers!

Don't miss Rob Parsons, author of *Teenagers! What every parent has to know*, exploring the ups and downs of parenting teens:

* Unravel the secrets of communicating with your teenager

* Understand why your teenager acts the way they do

* Discover vital keys for dealing with a testing teenager

If you're still searching for answers to the challenges of parenting a teenager, then you need to come and hear Rob Parsons at:

Teenagers! What every parent has to know in a town near you

Visit www.careforthefamily.org.uk/teenagers to find your nearest venue.

Teenagers! What every parent has to know events are organised by national charity Care for the Family.

Further information is available from **Care for the Family, Garth House, Freepost (CF4636), Cardiff CF15 7GZ,** by phone on **(029) 2081 0800** or online at **www.careforthefamily.org.uk**

Get to grips with family life today with Rob Parsons on DVD

21st Century Marriage and *21st Century Parent* are two brand new DVD-based courses featuring Rob Parsons, from national charity Care for the Family.

If you've ever wondered how to improve your relationship, or be the best parent you possibly can, Rob's down-to-earth style will support you in your family life.

21st Century Marriage includes:
* Knowing we matter
* Dealing with debt
* Love in the real world

21st Century Parent includes:
* You're not alone
* Defending the boundaries
* Teenagers!

With an accessible workbook to each DVD, you'll find these resources invaluable as you cope with the pressures of family life in the 21st Century.

To order your copy, call Care for the Family on **(029) 2081 0800** or order online at **www.careforthefamily.org.uk/21C**

Also by Rob Parsons:

The Sixty Minute Father
An Hour to Change Your Child's Life

*'A book that helps you achieve the most
important success of all'* Sir John Harvey-Jones

Rob Parsons establishes goals to help every father
ensure that he doesn't miss out on the greatest
opportunity of his life.

ISBN 978 0 340 630402
Also available on audio CD ISBN 978 1844 560004

The Sixty Minute Mother
A wonderful, witty book on the wisdom of motherhood

'Every mother should read this book – it's fantastic!'
Diane Louise Jordan

Talking to a variety of mothers from all backgrounds and
situations Rob has compiled a wonderfully inspirational
book on the highs and lows of being a mother.

ISBN 978 0 340 630617
Also available on Audio cassette ISBN 978 1840 325034

The Sixty Minute Marriage
'Wise and witty. Full of down-to-earth advice that works.'
Lynda Lee Potter

A simple book that will revolutionise your relationship.
Rob gives good, practical advice that will help every couple.

ISBN 978 0 340 671450

H
HODDER

www.madaboutbooks.co.uk

The Heart of Success

Making it in business without losing in life

'This book redefines the concept of success. It has some answers for people who are succeeding in business but are beginning to ask themselves whether there is more to life than they are currently achieving. It could change your life if you dare act on the thoughts it raises for you. I would recommend CEOs give this book to every manager in their company'
Jim Smith, Vice-President, HR, SmithKline Beecham R&D

'Rob Parsons is one of the most inspirational speakers in the country today. *The Heart of Success* has the same ingredients as his presentations – motivating, practical and giving you a sense that somebody has just turned on a light on.'
Rosemary Conley, author, broadcaster and Chairman of The Rosemary Conley Group

The Heart of Success is hard to put down and impossible to ignore. It has the ability not just to improve the performance of your company but your life as well.
Chris Street, Vice President and General Manager of Global Customer Services, Alcatel

For further information visit: www.letsdolife.com

ISBN 978 0 340 78623 9
Also available on audio CD ISBN 978 184032 509 6

H
HODDER

www.madaboutbooks.co.uk

229

The Money Secret

'Not just a book on debt – but on life choices.
This is unmissable.'
*Anthony Elliot, Former Chief Risk Officer,
Abbey National plc*

Practical and life-changing, *The Money Secret* will
totally revolutionise your attitude to money and
show how it can either be a source of freedom and
happiness or a burden of guilt and debt. As well as
offering solutions, this book challenges the status
quo and questions current spending habits. Rich or
poor, we have all at some time felt in despair about
money and its power over our lives. Rob Parsons
shows a new way forward that will change your life,
focus your priorities and put you back in control.

ISBN 978 0 340 862773
Also available on audio CD ISBN 978 1 844 560035

HODDER

www.madaboutbooks.co.uk